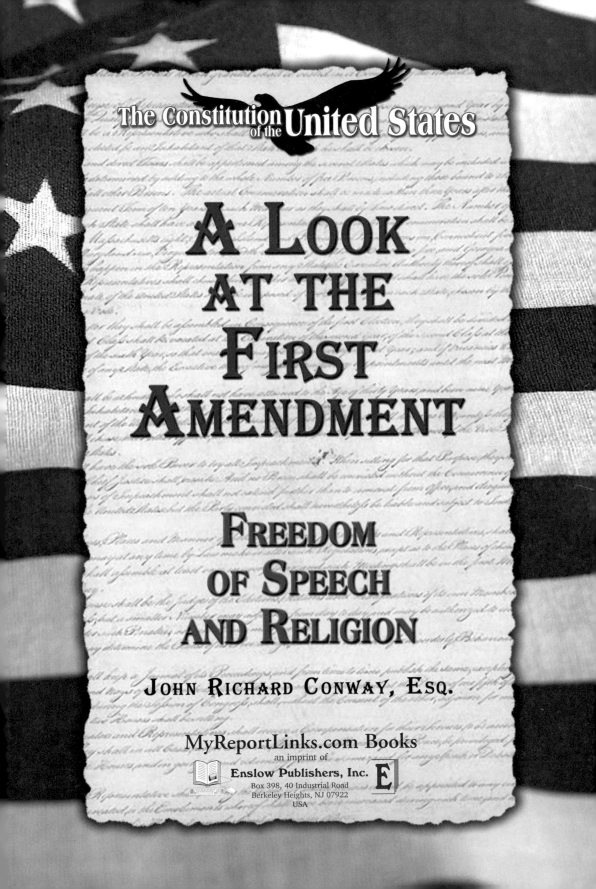

The Constitution
of the United States

A LOOK
AT THE
FIRST
AMENDMENT

FREEDOM
OF SPEECH
AND RELIGION

JOHN RICHARD CONWAY, ESQ.

MyReportLinks.com Books

an imprint of

Enslow Publishers, Inc. **E**

Box 398, 40 Industrial Road
Berkeley Heights, NJ 07922
USA

Library of Congress Cataloging-in-Publication Data

Conway, John Richard, 1969–
   A look at the First Amendment : freedom of speech and religion/John Richard
Conway.
      p. cm. — (The Constitution of the United States)
   Includes bibliographical references and index.
   ISBN-13: 978-1-59845-069-9 (hardcover)
   ISBN-10: 1-59845-069-7 (hardcover)
   1. United States. Constitution. 1st Amendment—Juvenile literature. 2. Freedom of
expression—United States—Juvenile literature. 3. Freedom of religion—United States—
Juvenile literature. I. Title.
KF4770.Z9C66 2008
342.7308'5—dc22

                            2007019731

Printed in the United States of America

10 9 8 7 6 5 4 3 2 1

To Our Readers:
Through the purchase of this book, you and your library gain access to the Report Links that specifically back
up this book.
The Publisher will provide access to the Report Links that back up this book and will keep these Report Links
up to date on **www.myreportlinks.com** for five years from the book's first publication date.
We have done our best to make sure all Internet addresses in this book were active and appropriate when we
went to press. However, the author and the Publisher have no control over, and assume no liability for, the
material available on those Internet sites or on other Web sites they may link to.
The usage of the MyReportLinks.com Books Web site is subject to the terms and conditions stated on the Usage
Policy Statement on **www.myreportlinks.com**.
A password may be required to access the Report Links that back up this book. The password is found on the
bottom of page 4 of this book.
Any comments or suggestions can be sent by e-mail to comments@myreportlinks.com or to the address on the
back cover.

♻ Enslow Publishers, Inc. is committed to printing our books on recycled paper. The paper in every book
contains between 10% to 30% post-consumer waste (PCW). The cover board on the outside of each book
contains 100% PCW. Our goal is to do our part to help young people and the environment too!

Photo Credits: Alliance Defense Fund, p. 44; American Civil Liberties Union, p. 71; American Library
Association, p. 12; Americans United for Separation of Church and State, p. 36; Anti-Defamation League,
p. 47; AP/Wide World Photos, p. 91; The Center for Education Reform, p. 100; ChillingEffects.com, p. 86;
Digital Stock Photos: Government and Social Issues, pp. 108–109; Emory University, p. 25; Federal
Communications Commission, p. 82; FindLaw, pp. 33, 81; First Amendment Center, p. 106; Library of
Congress, pp. 17, 19, 21, 22, 24, 52, 66, 67, 69, 76, 83, 98; MyReportLinks.com Books, p. 4; National Archives,
pp. 27, 29; National Education Association, p. 97; National Security Archive, p. 92; Privacy.org, p. 85; The
Rutherford Institute, p. 88; Shutterstock.com, pp. 9, 16, 34–35, 37, 40–41, 60–61, 74–75, 78–79; Supreme
Court of the United States, p. 99; The Supreme Court Historical Society, p. 56; University of Groningen, p. 26;
University of Missouri-Kansas City, pp. 11, 77; U.S. Department of State, p. 105; U.S. Government Printing
Office, p. 103; U.S. Supreme Court Media, p. 68; The White House, pp. 30, 48; Yale University, p. 18.

Cover Photo: Shutterstock: Statue of Liberty

CONTENTS

MyReportLinks.com Books
Great Books, Great Links, Great for Research!

The Internet sites featured in this book can save you hours of research time. These Internet sites—we call them **"Report Links"**—are constantly changing, but we keep them up to date on our Web site.

When you see this "Approved Web Site" logo, you will know that we are directing you to a great Internet site that will help you with your research.

Give it a try! Type http://www.myreportlinks.com into your browser, click on the series title and enter the password, then click on the book title, and scroll down to the Report Links listed for this book.

The Report Links will bring you to great source documents, photographs, and illustrations. MyReportLinks.com Books save you time, feature Report Links that are kept up to date, and make report writing easier than ever! A complete listing of the Report Links can be found on pages 118–119 at the back of the book.

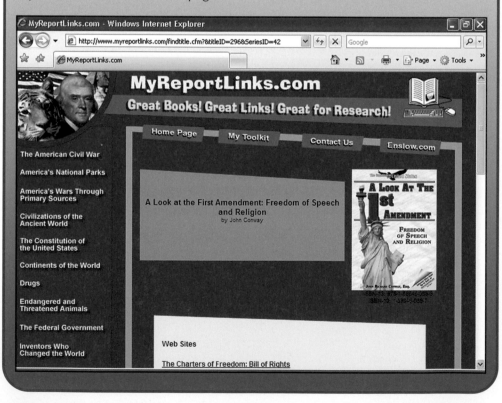

Please see "To Our Readers" on the copyright page for important information about this book, the MyReportLinks.com Web site, and the Report Links that back up this book.

Please enter **FAC1556** if asked for a password.

TIME LINE

1606 —The case *De Libellis Famosis* defines seditious libel in English Law.

1689 —The English Bill of Rights is passed by England's Parliament.

1735 —The Peter Zenger trial ends, in a verdict of not guilty, ushering in a new American sense of freedom of the press.

1775 —The American Revolution begins.

1776 —The Virginia Bill of Rights, written by George Mason, is adopted.

July 4: The Declaration of Independence is adopted.

1777 —Congress approves the Articles of Confederation.

1779 —Thomas Jefferson drafts the Statute of Religious Freedom.

1787 —Delegates meet in Philadelphia, Pennsylvania, to modify the Articles of Confederation.

1787 —The new United States Constitution is created.

1789 —The First United States Congress is seated and is directed to draft a Bill of Rights.

1791 —Virginia becomes the eleventh state to ratify the Bill of Rights, effectively making it the first ten amendments to the United States Constitution.

1798 —Congress passes the Alien and Sedition Acts.

1833 —In *Barron* v. *Baltimore,* the U.S. Supreme Court determines that state governments are not bound by the Fifth Amendment's requirement for just compensation in cases of eminent domain.

1919 —Justice Oliver Wendell Holmes finds that some forms of speech are not protected by the First Amendment. For example, words or speech that present "a clear and present danger," such as when a person falsely shouts "fire" in a crowded theater, are not protected by the First Amendment.

1925— The case of *Gitlow* v. *New York* partially reverses the U.S. Supreme Court's decision in *Barron* v. *Baltimore,* meaning that the Bill of Rights applies to the actions of the individual states.

1947— The Supreme Court issues its finding in *Everson* v. *Board of Education,* a ruling that established the judicial principle of 'a wall of separation between Church and State.'

1963— In *Abington Township School District* v. *Schemp,* the Supreme Court rules that reading the Bible in public school violates the Establishment Clause and its principle that government should not support any particular religion.

1971— Chief Justice Warren Burger establishes the three-pronged "Lemon Test," a set of standards used to determine if a law violates the First Amendment's Establishment Clause. Burger's test is still used today to analyze the legality of a statute.

1985— The Court extends its finding in Abington when it rules in *Wallace* v. *Jaffree* that an Alabama law requiring a moment of silence for prayer or meditation in a public school is not allowed.

1989—The Supreme Court overturned a Texas law that criminalized the burning of the American flag, arguing that, though offensive to some, flag burning is a form of protected speech.

THE FIRST AMENDMENT IN ACTION

O n December 2, 2004, the *San Francisco Chronicle,* a California newspaper, printed a story that asserted that some of the most prominent players in Major League Baseball had taken steroids and other performance-enhancing drugs. The reporters who wrote the story, Mark Fainaru-Wada and Lance Williams, got the information for their story from testimony given before a grand jury.

Under normal circumstances, testimony given to a grand jury remains secret. In other words, whoever told the reporters that Jason Giambi and Barry Bonds (two of the players named in the *Chronicle* story) took illegal drugs broke the law. Nevertheless, sometimes secret information leaks out. In this case, Fainaru-Wada and Williams had a source—a person who had access to the secret testimony and revealed its contents to them. In spite of the fact they had obtained their information illegally, Fainaru-Wada and Williams believed they had a duty to inform the public. So the reporters wrote the story for the newspaper.

Given how important sports in general and major league baseball in particular are to the American public, it is no surprise that the *Chronicle's* story had a huge impact. Indeed, the reporting done by Fainaru-Wada and Williams forced baseball to confront the role illegal drugs have played in the game in the last few decades. In December 2007, the U.S. Congress released the contents of the Mitchell Report, a 409-page study that went well beyond the reporting done by the *Chronicle* and firmly established that baseball had a serious drug problem.

But the *San Francisco Chronicle's* story was not important just because it forced Major League Baseball officials to change the way they dealt with athletes taking illegal drugs. It was important because it brought into question the Constitutional principle of freedom of the press.

AFTERMATH

More than a year after their story ran, Fainaru-Wada and Williams were asked to testify before another grand jury to explain how they gained access to secret testimony. The reporters refused, citing the need to protect the identity of their source. Finally, on September 21, 2006, a federal judge ordered the reporters to reveal the name of their source. If they still refused, the judge threatened to send them to jail for up to eighteen months. They refused.

Though neither Fainaru-Wada, the father of two children, nor Williams wanted to go to jail, both understood the importance of their decision. They were prepared to go to jail for a long time to protect what they believed was their First Amendment right of freedom of the press.

The First Amendment does not explicitly guarantee anonymity to a reporter's source. However, over time, the courts have come to understand that the free flow of information is a key piece of a

Freedom of the Press, designed to ▶ encourage the free flow of ideas and information throughout society, is one of the First Amendment's most important principles.

democratic society. After all, information can uncover illegal activities, like the abuse of performance-enhancing drugs in major-league baseball. If a source, in this case the person who tipped off Fainaru-Wada and Williams, knew he might go to jail for providing information, the all-important free-flow of information would stop—and our democracy would be a little less secure.

"This is a public issue," said Fainaru-Wada, "the ability to get [unrestrained] information. The real danger is this, not the immediate danger of reporters going to jail. It is the much broader danger of a vastly less informed public."[1]

Fainaru-Wada and Williams avoided jail because the authorities identified the reporters' source without their help. And though many people applauded them for their willingness to sacrifice their freedom, Fainaru-Wada and Williams are just a recent example of people who have put themselves at risk for what they considered the greater good.

➔THE ZENGER TRIAL

In 1733, former New York Attorney General James Alexander asked John Peter Zenger to print America's first political party newspaper, the *New York Weekly Journal*.[2] Zenger, a printer by trade, agreed.

There is no way of knowing whether the thirty-seven-year-old Zenger agreed with the material he printed in the *New York Weekly Journal,* or whether he was simply doing a job for a paying client. Nevertheless, as the printer, Zenger—and not the author of the material in the paper—was responsible for his newspaper's content.

The *New York Weekly Journal* was financed by a New York political party that did not agree with the people in power in the government. Zenger's paper was very critical of New York Governor William Cosby; one article accused him of rigging elections, stealing money and land. Another accused the governor of being a traitor.

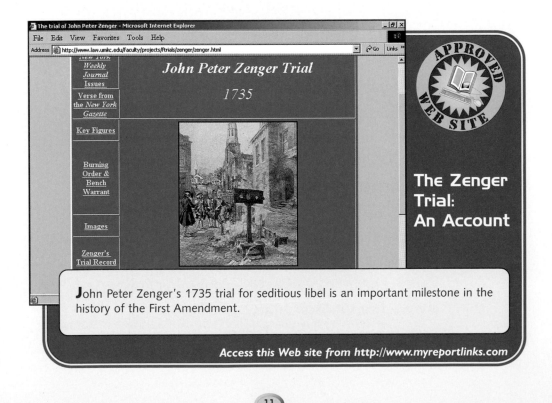

John Peter Zenger's 1735 trial for seditious libel is an important milestone in the history of the First Amendment.

Access this Web site from http://www.myreportlinks.com

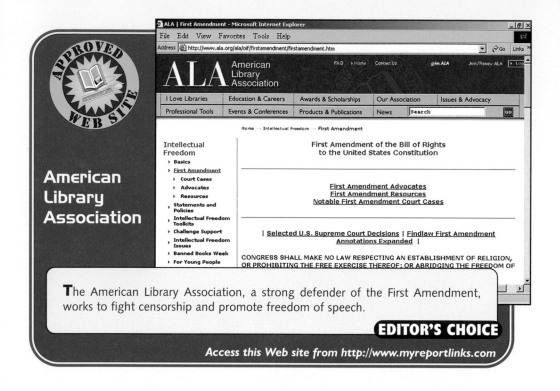

The American Library Association, a strong defender of the First Amendment, works to fight censorship and promote freedom of speech.

EDITOR'S CHOICE

Access this Web site from http://www.myreportlinks.com

Finally, Governor Cosby had had enough and on November 17, 1734, Zenger was arrested. His bail was set at £400 pounds. The large amount won Zenger a lot of sympathy in the community.[3]

At first, it looked like Zenger's trial was fixed and he would lose. The printer's first two lawyers were rejected by the court after they objected to the fact that Zenger would be tried by two judges—both hand-picked by Cosby—rather than by a jury. Zenger's friends and supporters hired Andrew Hamilton, an elderly and highly respected lawyer from Philadelphia.

When it was decided that Zenger would have a jury trial, Governor Cosby submitted a list of potential jurors, including some of his former associates, all of whom would be sympathetic to his case.

Rather than dispute that Zenger had published defamatory statements about Governor Cosby, Hamilton rose before the jury and argued:

> The question before the Court and you, Gentlemen of the Jury, is not of small nor private concern. It is not the Cause of a poor Printer. . . . It is the Cause of Liberty. And I make no Doubt [but that]. . . every Man, who prefers Freedom to a Life of Slavery will bless and honor You, as men who have baffled the Attempt of Tyranny, and by an impartial and uncorrupt Verdict have laid a noble Foundation for securing to ourselves . . . that, to which Nature and the Laws of our Country have given us a Right— the Liberty both of exposing and opposing arbitrary Power . . . by speaking and writing Truth.[4]

→ NOT GUILTY

On August 4, 1735, after a short trial, Zenger was found not guilty on the charge of publishing "seditious libels," or the crime of spreading hate for a government institution or officer. Hamilton had successfully argued that Zenger's articles were not "libelous" because they were based on fact and that libel only exists when lies are presented as the truth. In other words, Hamilton argued, the truth can never be libelous.

The verdict was surprising: on the one hand, because Governor Cosby had chosen the judges, and second, because it broke with English legal tradition, which held that truth was not a defense for the English common law crime of seditious libel. However it was reached, the verdict in the Zenger case quickly became the cornerstone for the foundation of American freedom of the press and freedom of expression.

THE ORIGINS OF THE AMENDMENT

2

*T*he notion of freedom, the sense that no one can tell us as Americans what we can and cannot do, runs very deep in all of us. From the earliest age, we are reminded that America was founded on the principle of freedom—pilgrims came to this new world in the seventeenth century in part because they wanted to be free to practice their own religion and to escape the harsh rule of Britain's king. We are taught to sing that this is "the land of the free" because America has always had a tradition of free expression.

Before separating from Britain, the United States was a group of thirteen colonies on the eastern seaboard. A few of these colonies—Massachusetts Bay, settled by Puritans, Pennsylvania, settled by Quakers, and Maryland, which was intended to be a Roman Catholic colony—were established so that people could freely express their religion.

People came to America from Britain because they wanted religious freedom. In seventeenth-century Britain, the Church of England (later known in the United States as the Episcopal Church) was the only

The Declaration of Independence, written in 1776 by men like (from left) Ben Franklin, John Adams, and Thomas Jefferson, was an expression of the colonists' desire to be free of the king's interference and free to determine their own futures.

religion that people were allowed to practice. All British citizens were required by law to belong to the Church of England. All other religious beliefs were, technically, illegal. In fact, throughout Europe, most countries had an established religion, supported and in many cases *mandated* by the government. France and Spain were Catholic countries, while Germany had been fighting a long and brutal series of religious wars between various German rulers who were Protestant and Roman Catholic.

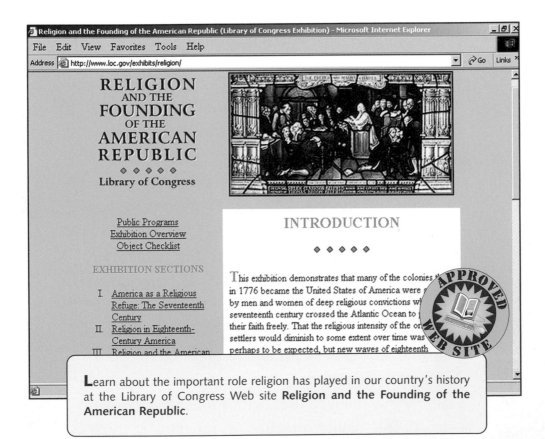

Learn about the important role religion has played in our country's history at the Library of Congress Web site **Religion and the Founding of the American Republic**.

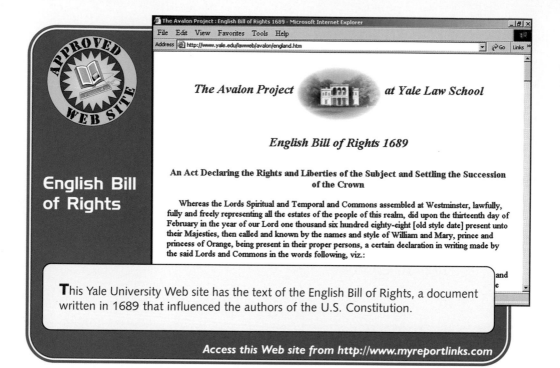

Access this Web site from http://www.myreportlinks.com

The Avalon Project : English Bill of Rights 1689 - Microsoft Internet Explorer

File   Edit   View   Favorites   Tools   Help

Address   http://www.yale.edu/lawweb/avalon/england.htm   Go   Links

The Avalon Project   *at Yale Law School*

English Bill of Rights 1689

An Act Declaring the Rights and Liberties of the Subject and Settling the Succession of the Crown

Whereas the Lords Spiritual and Temporal and Commons assembled at Westminster, lawfully, fully and freely representing all the estates of the people of this realm, did upon the thirteenth day of February in the year of our Lord one thousand six hundred eighty-eight [old style date] present unto their Majesties, then called and known by the names and style of William and Mary, prince and princess of Orange, being present in their proper persons, a certain declaration in writing made by the said Lords and Commons in the words following, viz.:

English Bill of Rights

This Yale University Web site has the text of the English Bill of Rights, a document written in 1689 that influenced the authors of the U.S. Constitution.

But European rulers did not stop at religion—speech was similarly regulated. In 1606, the case of *De Libellis Famosis* defined seditious libel in English law as criticism of the government, public persons, or the king. Britain further controlled verbal expression by limiting the press through a complex system that prohibited any publication from being distributed without a government license.

By the period leading up to the Revolution, most American colonies had established religions, though most also had documents that expressed support for the idea of religious toleration (meaning people could practice a religion of their

ARTICLES

OF

CONFEDERATION

AND

PERPETUAL UNION

BETWEEN THE

STATES

OF

NEW-HAMPSHIRE, MASSACHUSETTS-BAY, RHODE-ISLAND AND PROVIDENCE PLANTATIONS, CONNECTICUT, NEW-YORK, NEW-JERSEY, PENNSYLVANIA, DELAWARE, MARYLAND, VIRGINIA, NORTH CAROLINA, SOUTH CAROLINA AND GEORGIA.

WILLIAMSBURG:
Printed by J. DIXON & W. HUNTER.
M,DCC,LXXVIII.

The Articles of Confederation, written in 1777, were intended to be a governing framework for the United States of America. However, as America grew, it became clear the country needed a stronger framework and in 1788, the Articles were replaced by the U.S. Constitution.

choosing). Despite these restrictions, the colonists also had a custom of personal liberty that they had inherited from Great Britain.

In fact, as early as 1689, the British Parliament passed a Bill of Rights that limited the king or a queen's power to a certain extent. In theory, this Bill of Rights prevented royal interference in the courts, prevented the king from taxing the public at will, and eliminated the existence of a peace-time standing army without the consent of the government. The English Bill of Rights also established certain liberties that would sound familiar to modern Americans, such as protection against cruel and unusual punishment or from being forced to forfeit property or paying fines without trial (also called due process).[1]

➲ THE SECOND CONTINENTAL CONGRESS

After the American Revolution ended in 1783, the thirteen states operated under the Articles of Confederation. In 1777, the Second Continental Congress had established the Articles as a means of providing a central government for the thirteen independent states of Massachusetts, New Hampshire, Rhode Island, Connecticut, New York, New Jersey, Pennsylvania, Delaware, Maryland, Virginia, North Carolina, South Carolina, and Georgia. While the Articles were adequate in certain respects, they were not a strong enough framework with which to run a large and diverse country.

Realizing they needed something stronger, representatives from twelve of the thirteen colonies met in Philadelphia in the spring of 1787; their goal was to modify the existing Articles. That is, most of the delegates intended only to change the Articles slightly, not develop an entirely new document. But after a few months, the delegates, led by George Washington, had devised an entirely new form of government. The document that came to be known as the Constitution envisioned a legislative branch (represented by the Congress), a chief executive (the President), and an independent judiciary (the Supreme Court).

This form of government was closely based on the state

One of this country's Founding ▶ *Fathers and the first chief justice of the U.S. Supreme Court, John Jay co-wrote* The Federalist Papers, *a series of essays written to influence public opinion and build support for the Constitution.*

constitution James Madison had helped draft for Virginia in 1776. It was also very controversial, mainly because it advocated a strong central government, something that reminded many people of the king and the long war they had recently fought to escape his overwhelming power. Men like Alexander Hamilton, John Jay, and James Madison who supported the new constitution were called "Federalists." These men lobbied their state legislatures for passage of the new constitution and even wrote a series of powerful essays in support of it. *The Federalist Papers* were originally printed only in New York newspapers, but they were eventually printed throughout the thirteen colonies.[2]

◀ *James Madison, sometimes referred to as the "Father of the Constitution," helped draft Virginia's constitution in 1776 and was a leading author of The Federalist Papers.*

Opponents of the Constitution were concerned that the new government would be too strong and that it would have too much power over the individual states. They were quick to remind people that Americans had fought a long, difficult war to guarantee their liberty from an all-powerful king. Now the Federalists were proposing a strong central government that many feared could be just as effective an instrument of tyranny as any king. Anti-Federalists demanded that the new constitution contain a "bill of rights" to protect individual freedom and liberty.

➔ THE FEDERALIST PAPERS

The Federalists argued that a bill of rights was unnecessary—the constitution was a structure for a government, and no private rights or liberties had been surrendered to create that structure. In Federalist Paper #84, Alexander Hamilton argued that listing individual rights would, in effect, limit the number of rights an individual had to those that were specifically listed. In other words, any right *not* spelled out and defined would then be controlled by government. Any list of specific rights would, in effect become the only rights an individual had. Hamilton wrote:

> I go further, and affirm that bills of rights . . . are not only unnecessary in the proposed constitution, but would even be dangerous. They would contain

One of the most important men in colonial America, Alexander Hamilton was one of George Washington's top aides in the Revolutionary War, co-wrote The Federalist Papers and became the first secretary of the treasury under President Washington.

various exceptions to powers which are not granted; and on this very account, would afford a colorable pretext to claim more than were granted. . . . Why for instance, should it be said, that the liberty of the press shall not be restrained, when no power is given by which restrictions may be imposed?"[3]

The Anti-Federalists were unimpressed. A Massachusetts Anti-Federalist, writing under the pseudonym "John DeWitt," argued:

A people, entering into society, surrender such a part of their natural rights, as shall be necessary

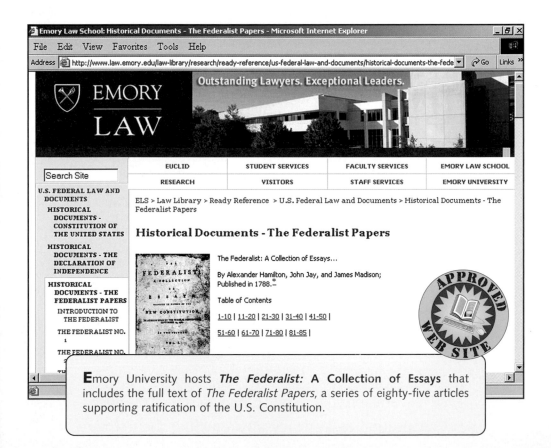

Emory University hosts *The Federalist: A Collection of Essays* that includes the full text of *The Federalist Papers*, a series of eighty-five articles supporting ratification of the U.S. Constitution.

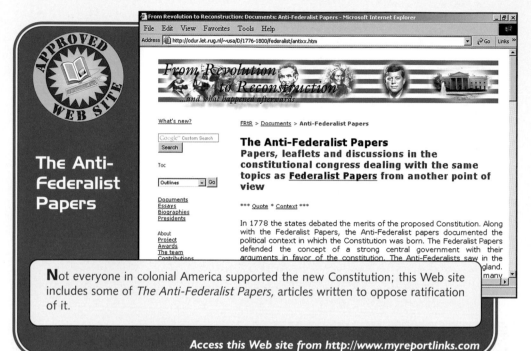

From Revolution to Reconstruction: Documents: Anti-Federalist Papers - Microsoft Internet Explorer

File   Edit   View   Favorites   Tools   Help

Address http://odur.let.rug.nl/~usa/D/1776-1800/federalist/antixx.htm

From Revolution to Reconstruction
...and what happened afterwards

What's new?

FRtR > Documents > Anti-Federalist Papers

The Anti-Federalist Papers
Papers, leaflets and discussions in the
constitutional congress dealing with the same
topics as **Federalist Papers** from another point of
view

Toc

Outlines

Documents
Essays
Biographies
Presidents

About
Project
Awards
The team
Contributions

*** Quote * Context ***

In 1778 the states debated the merits of the proposed Constitution. Along
with the Federalist Papers, the Anti-Federalist papers documented the
political context in which the Constitution was born. The Federalist Papers
defended the concept of a strong central government with their
arguments in favor of the constitution. The Anti-Federalists saw in the

**The Anti-
Federalist
Papers**

Not everyone in colonial America supported the new Constitution; this Web site
includes some of *The Anti-Federalist Papers,* articles written to oppose ratification
of it.

Access this Web site from http://www.myreportlinks.com

for the existence of that society. They [rights] are
so precious in themselves, that they would never
be parted with, did not the preservation of the
remainder require it. . . . That a Constitution for
the United States does not require a Bill of Rights,
when it is considered that a Constitution for an
individual State would, I cannot conceive. The difference between them is only in the numbers of the
parties concerned; they are both a compact
between the Governors and Governed, the letter
of which must be adhered to in discussing their
powers. That which is not expressly granted, is of
course retained.[4]

Several smaller states had ratified the new
Constitution as a means of protecting their rights

and political powers, but key states incuding Massachusetts, Virginia, and New York had not ratified the document yet. Without their support, the Constitution had no chance of being accepted as the framework for a new form of government. Massachusetts had a strong Anti-Federalist party, but it was largely leaderless because prominent opponents like Samuel Adams and Elbridge Gerry had personal reasons for not wanting to publicly oppose the new Constitution.

Adams represented Boston, the area of the state most in favor of ratifying the Constitution.

The National Archives hosts **The Charters of Freedom: Bill of Rights,** which includes a copy of the first ten Amendments to the Constitution.

EDITOR'S CHOICE

He did not want to alienate voters and possibly lose his seat in the legislature. And Gerry was one of the main authors of the Constitution, and though he did not sign the document, he also did not want to speak out against it. That made John Hancock the key Anti-Federalist in Massachusetts. However, Hancock was an ambitious politician, and he was persuaded to throw his support behind the new document—Virginia had not ratified the Constitution, and the Federalists in Massachusetts dangled the possibility of the vice-presidency to Hancock. There was even the slim possibility that, with Virginia (and George Washington) out of the picture, Hancock might be made president. Hancock dropped his opposition and Massachusetts ratified the Constitution on February 6, 1788.

SUBJECT TO APPROVAL

However, Massachusetts' support was conditioned on some changes to the Constitution. Specifically, Massachusetts demanded that the Constitution include some statement of personal rights. Ratification with conditions became a new weapon in the Federalist arsenal, and the agreement to amend the Constitution with a bill of rights became known as the "Massachusetts Compromise."[5] With the compromise in place, most other states quickly ratified the Constitution.

NARA | The National Archives Experience - Microsoft Internet Explorer

File   Edit   View   Favorites   Tools   Help

Address 🖉 http://www.archives.gov/national-archives-experience/charters/virginia_declaration_of_rights.html   ⌐ Go   Links »

THE NATIONAL ARCHIVES EXPERIENCE

| MAIN PAGE | VISIT US | CHARTERS OF FREEDOM | NEWS AND EVENTS | SUPPORT THE ARCHIVES |

MAKING OF THE CHARTERS   THE DECLARATION OF INDEPENDENCE   THE CONSTITUTION   THE BILL OF RIGHTS   IMPACT OF THE CHARTERS   HIGH-RESOLUTION IMAGES

the *Charters of Freedom*
"A NEW WORLD IS AT HAND"

MAKING OF THE CHARTERS   IMPACT OF THE CHARTERS

◄ back

Bill of Rights
THE VIRGINIA DECLARATION OF RIGHTS

America's Bill of Rights was based on The Virginia Declaration of Rights, which was written in 1776 by George Mason.

The Virginia Declaration of Rights

APPROVED WEB SITE

Access this Web site from http://www.myreportlinks.com

On March 4, 1789, the first U.S. Congress met in New York City. Its first order of business was to draft a bill of rights. James Madison began drafting the document that would become the Bill of Rights, which he based on the Virginia Declaration of Rights that was written in 1776 by fellow Virginian George Mason. Both, in turn, were based in part on the English Bill of Rights of 1689. Madison also drew from the Virginia Statute for Religious Freedom drafted in 1779 by his close friend Thomas Jefferson, which stated:

"No man shall be compelled to . . . support any religious worship, place, or ministry whatsoever, nor shall . . . otherwise suffer, on account of his

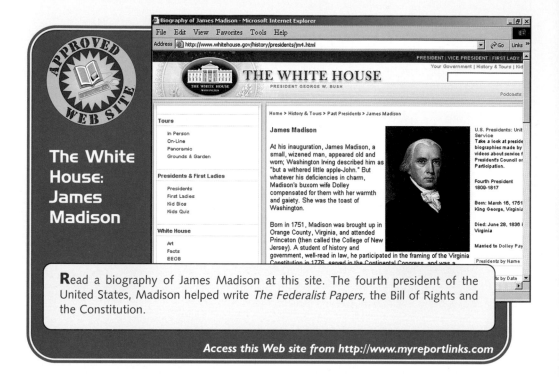

The White House: James Madison

Biography of James Madison - Microsoft Internet Explorer

File   Edit   View   Favorites   Tools   Help

Address http://www.whitehouse.gov/history/presidents/jm4.html   Go   Links »

PRESIDENT | VICE PRESIDENT | FIRST LADY |

THE WHITE HOUSE

THE WHITE HOUSE WASHINGTON   PRESIDENT GEORGE W. BUSH

Your Government | History & Tours | Kid

Podcasts

Home > History & Tours > Past Presidents > James Madison

Tours
In Person
On-Line
Panoramic
Grounds & Garden

Presidents & First Ladies
Presidents
First Ladies
Kid Bios
Kids Quiz

White House
Art
Facts
EEOB

James Madison

At his inauguration, James Madison, a small, wizened man, appeared old and worn; Washington Irving described him as "but a withered little apple-John." But whatever his deficiencies in charm, Madison's buxom wife Dolley compensated for them with her warmth and gaiety. She was the toast of Washington.

Born in 1751, Madison was brought up in Orange County, Virginia, and attended Princeton (then called the College of New Jersey). A student of history and government, well-read in law, he participated in the framing of the Virginia Constitution in 1776, served in the Continental Congress, and was a

U.S. Presidents: Unit Service
Take a look at preside biographies made by videos about service f President's Council or Participation.

Fourth President
1809-1817

Born: March 16, 1751
King George, Virginia

Died: June 28, 1836 I
Virginia

Married to Dolley Pay

Presidents by Name

s by Date

Read a biography of James Madison at this site. The fourth president of the United States, Madison helped write *The Federalist Papers,* the Bill of Rights and the Constitution.

Access this Web site from http://www.myreportlinks.com

religious opinions or belief; but that all men shall be free . . . in matters of religion. . . ."[6]

On June 8, 1789, Madison introduced his twelve articles on the floor of Congress. On November 20, 1789, New Jersey became the first state to ratify the articles as amendments to the Constitution, though it rejected Article II, as did New Hampshire, New York, Pennsylvania, and Rhode Island. Maryland and North Carolina followed suit about one month later. When Virginia became the eleventh state to ratify on December 15, 1791, ten of the twelve articles, known as the Bill of Rights, became the first ten amendments to the Constitution.

While the amendments went into effect as part of the U.S. Constitution in 1789, Connecticut, Massachusetts, and Georgia did not officially ratify the amendments until 1939, the 150th anniversary of the Bill of Rights.

When it was first ratified, the Bill of Rights only applied to federal government actions. While Madison had always intended to have it apply to the states, that language was removed. Indeed, it was not until 1868 and the passage of the Fourteenth Amendment that the Bill of Rights was extended to the states.

3 THE AMENDMENT UP CLOSE

"Congress shall make no law respecting an establishment of religion, or prohibiting the free exercise thereof; or abridging the freedom of speech, or of the press; or the right of the people peaceably to assemble, and to petition the Government for a redress of grievances."

The First Amendment is brief, but it covers a tremendous amount of legal ground and incorporates some of our most fundamental rights as citizens.

→ THE RELIGIOUS CLAUSES

"Congress shall make no law respecting an establishment of religion, or prohibiting the free exercise thereof."

These words make up what are known as the establishment clause and the free exercise clause, collectively known as the religious clauses. These words define the relationship between church and state in the United States.

→THE ESTABLISHMENT CLAUSE

The establishment clause—*"Congress shall make no law respecting an establishment of religion"*—is interpreted to mean that government can have no active role in religion. Government cannot establish a national church or require attendance at or support of a single national church or religion. Furthermore, government cannot favor or support any one religious or nonreligious belief system over another. While this clause was initially interpreted only as it related to the federal government, it was later expanded to include all state and local government action as well.

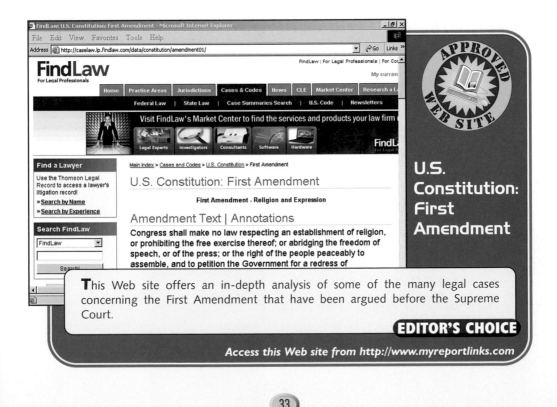

This Web site offers an in-depth analysis of some of the many legal cases concerning the First Amendment that have been argued before the Supreme Court.

EDITOR'S CHOICE

Access this Web site from http://www.myreportlinks.com

→Free Exercise Clause

"Congress shall make no law respecting an establishment of religion, or prohibiting the free exercise thereof."

The rights granted by this section are generally conceded to be a right to believe and a right to act.

The government cannot interfere with a person's right to believe; all Americans are allowed to hold whatever religious beliefs and opinions that they wish. However, the state may limit the right to act on religious belief if it has a compelling reason to do so. This limitation usually centers on the performance of specific religious practices that the government considers to be bad for the community, such as human sacrifice or polygamy (being married to more than one person at the same time).

➡ THE FREEDOM OF SPEECH

"Congress shall make no law. . . abridging the freedom of speech. . . ."

Perhaps the broadest right guaranteed to all Americans is the freedom of speech—the right of every American to express thoughts and opinions.

Though it begins simply—"We the People"— the U.S. Constitution embodies some of mankind's highest ideals. More than 220 years after it was written, it remains one of the most important documents in the world.

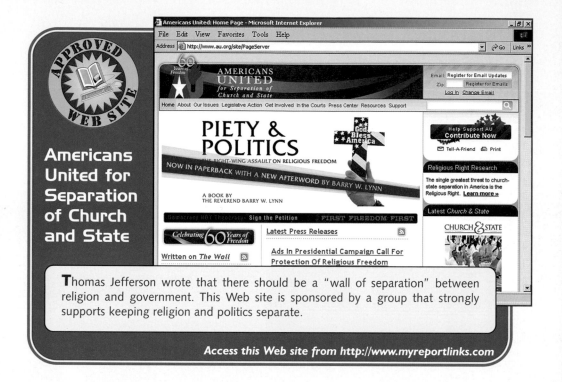

Americans United for Separation of Church and State

Thomas Jefferson wrote that there should be a "wall of separation" between religion and government. This Web site is sponsored by a group that strongly supports keeping religion and politics separate.

Access this Web site from http://www.myreportlinks.com

Speech is not just the spoken word, but is accepted to include a wide range of expressive activity. Freedom of speech is only limited when it is weighed against very specific tests balancing that right against other liberties, such as protecting the community from immediate harm, or the use of untrue statements to harm others. In general, however, government is hesitant to prohibit *any* speech, no matter how controversial or offensive that speech may be to some.

➡THE FREEDOM OF THE PRESS

"Congress shall make no law . . . abridging the freedom of speech, or of the press. . . ."

"First Amendment" Expression Area

designated for the sale and distribution of printed matter in accordance with the provisions of 36 CFR 2.52 (A permit is required)

This area has been set aside for individuals or groups exercising their constitutional first amendment rights. The National Park Service neither encourages nor discourages, or otherwise endorses, these activities.

Permitted To Solicit Here Now

Despite the fact that the First Amendment encompasses many rights, to many Americans, its most important guarantee is the freedom to say whatever we want without fear of punishment.

Freedom of the press has limits similar to those regulating freedom of speech. That is, the right to say or publish something is weighed against the greater community good. The press—which today includes newspapers, television, movies, radio, and the Internet—has additional rules regarding taxation and content regulation.

The development of new technologies like the Internet has forced the courts to change their interpretation in some instances. For example, historically, the courts have been very hesitant to impose any restrictions on what the press can and cannot say. However, the courts have upheld some form of content restrictions based on the limited number of radio and television frequencies available—the theory being that there is no need for too many similar viewpoints to be broadcast over a small region. However, with the explosion of technologies, these technological limits on the freedom of the press will likely face new challenges.

➔THE RIGHT OF PEACEABLE ASSEMBLY

Freedom of assembly gives people the right to associate with any group or individual of their choosing, be it a political party, club, or organization. However, the right of free assembly is not guaranteed in every circumstance; there are rules in place that regulate things like time and place of assembly and which are intended to protect the greater public good.

For example, a group that wants to protest a government policy may be required to get a permit from local officials. This is done to make sure that there is adequate public space for the protest and enough protection for both the protesters and those being protested against.

THE RIGHT TO PETITION THE GOVERNMENT FOR REDRESS

"The right . . . to petition the government for redress" means that every individual and organization within the United States can bring legal action against or lobby (communicate directly) government officials to correct a government action. This clause ensures that individuals who take this action do not need to be afraid that the government will try to get revenge or punish an individual for daring to challenge the government.

COVERAGE OF THE AMENDMENT

While James Madison envisioned a time when the Bill of Rights would apply to all government action within the United States, the amendments as they were ratified contained no mention of state governments. Indeed, for many years, the U.S. Bill of Rights applied only to federal government actions, leaving states to act on their own and enforce their own bills of rights. For example, a number of states maintained

After all is said and done, it is left to the nine justices of the Supreme Court to determine what rights are protected by the First Amendment. The Supreme Court Building is shown here.

established churches, while others, like Maryland and New York, determined that the state could control speech and the press.

Two important cases helped shape the U.S. Supreme Court's interpretation of how the Bill of Rights and the Amendments impacted Americans' lives.

➲BARRON V. BALTIMORE

In the early nineteenth century, the government of Baltimore, Maryland, set out to improve its public works—repaving streets, building embankments, and redirecting some streams into Baltimore's harbor. When it rained, these streams carried sand and other waste into the harbor, making some of the wharves and docks along the waterfront unusable by certain ships. John Barron, who owned one of the wharfs that could no longer be used, sued the city of Baltimore. He argued that the Fifth Amendment and its clause that outlaws the taking of private property for public use "without just cause" should protect him and his business.

Barron won his case and the Baltimore County Court awarded him $4,500 in damages. The city appealed the verdict, which was overturned by the Maryland Court of Appeals. Barron then took his case to the U.S. Supreme Court.

When the case finally reached the Supreme Court in 1833, about ten years after Barron had originally sued, the court found that the Fifth Amendment only applied to situations involving the federal government, not state governments.[1] The end result of the Court's finding was that future courts took it to mean that since the Fifth Amendment did not apply to the states, none of the U.S. Bill of Rights could be applied to the various states. The outcome of *Barron* v. *Baltimore* established a legal precedent that stood for almost one hundred years.

➔GITLOW V. NEW YORK

Benjamin Gitlow was a communist who printed and distributed pamphlets that called for the violent overthrow of the U.S. government. In 1920, he was arrested and convicted under a New York state law that made it illegal to publish anything that advocated the overthrow of the government.

In *Gitlow* v. *New York* (1925), the U.S. Supreme Court agreed with the lower court and upheld Gitlow's conviction, determining that government can limit free speech in instances where a person or group is calling for the unlawful overthrow of government. Justice Edward Terry Sanford, writing for the majority, stated:

"For present purposes we may and do assume that freedom of speech and of the press—which are protected by the First Amendment from abridgment by Congress—are among the funda-

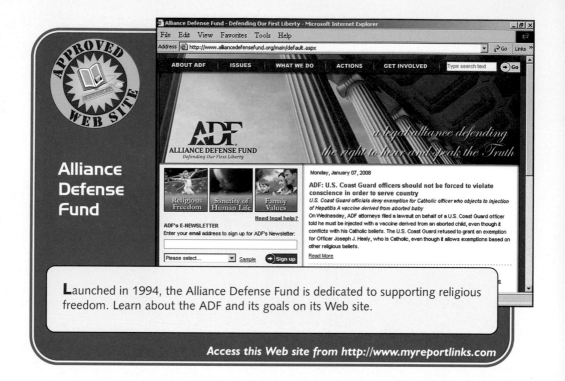

ABOUT ADF | ISSUES | WHAT WE DO | ACTIONS | GET INVOLVED | Type search text | Go

Alliance Defense Fund

Religious Freedom | Sanctity of Human Life | Family Values

Need legal help?

ADF's E-NEWSLETTER
Enter your email address to sign up for ADF's Newsletter:

Please select... | Sample | Sign up

Monday, January 07, 2008

ADF: U.S. Coast Guard officers should not be forced to violate conscience in order to serve country
U.S. Coast Guard officials deny exemption for Catholic officer who objects to injection of Hepatitis A vaccine derived from aborted baby
On Wednesday, ADF attorneys filed a lawsuit on behalf of a U.S. Coast Guard officer told he must be injected with a vaccine derived from an aborted child, even though it conflicts with his Catholic beliefs. The U.S. Coast Guard refused to grant an exemption for Officer Joseph J. Healy, who is Catholic, even though it allows exemptions based on other religious beliefs.
Read More

Alliance Defense Fund

Launched in 1994, the Alliance Defense Fund is dedicated to supporting religious freedom. Learn about the ADF and its goals on its Web site.

Access this Web site from http://www.myreportlinks.com

mental personal rights and 'liberties' protected by the due process clause of the Fourteenth Amendment from impairment by the States."[2] The due process clause states that the government may not take away a person's liberty or property without first giving that person a fair trial.

Gitlow v. *New York* was the first in a series of cases that, taken together, reversed the decision in *Barron* v. *Baltimore.* As a result of the decision in this case, courts began applying the United States Bill of Rights to all state and local government actions. This now forms the basis of the modern legal view of the application of the Bill of Rights.

SEPARATION OF CHURCH AND STATE 4

*T*he role of religion in American society has been and likely always will be one of serious debate and controversy. The United States was settled by people interested in pursuing a religion of their choice, not the king's. The Founding Fathers attempted to spell out the right of individuals to practice whatever religion they chose. Nevertheless, legal challenges to the religious clauses of the Constitution have been and continue to be heavily contested, as people or groups try to redefine the relationship and boundaries between church and state.

Immediately following the ratification of the Bill of Rights in 1791, many states continued the practice of having an official, established church. For example, at first Massachusetts recognized the Congregational Church. After 1780, Massachusetts law required all men to be members of a church of their choice, a requirement that was not abandoned until 1833. As late as 1877, New Hampshire required all members of the state legislature to be members of a Protestant church.

There has long been a struggle of ideology when addressing the religious clauses: Should there be complete separation of church and state or should the state make some accommodation for religion? Furthermore, there has been tension between the establishment clause and the free exercise clause, which has required continuous review of the balancing tests between the two clauses.

Here is a closer look at some of the most important legal cases dealing with religion and the controversial doctrine that says church and state must be separate.

FINANCIAL ASSISTANCE CASES

At the heart of many of the most serious controversies involving the establishment clause is whether religious organizations should be eligible to benefit from direct government funding.

Bradfield v. *Roberts,* the first challenge to the establishment clause heard by the U.S. Supreme Court, came more than one hundred years after the Bill of Rights was ratified. The court's ruling in the case demonstrates just how willing the court was to defer to state legislatures when it came to religious issues. In this instance, the question was

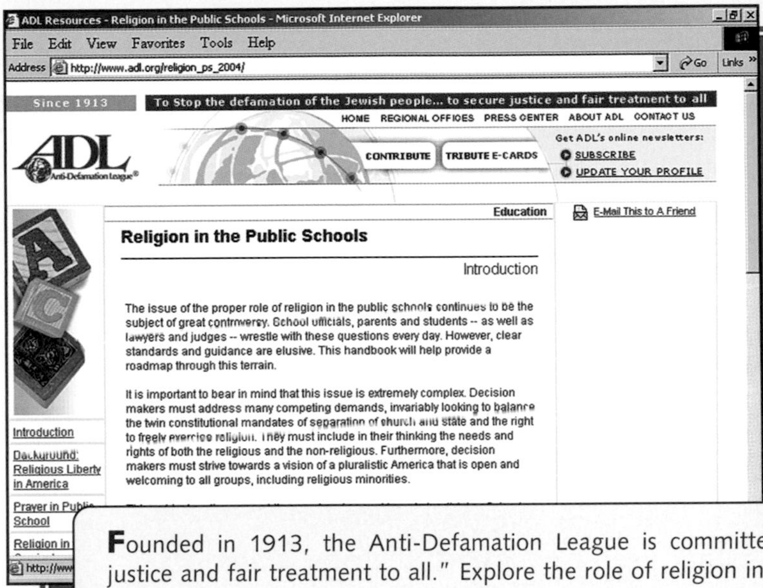
ADL Resources - Religion in the Public Schools - Microsoft Internet Explorer
File Edit View Favorites Tools Help
Address http://www.adl.org/religion_ps_2004/
Since 1913
To Stop the defamation of the Jewish people... to secure justice and fair treatment to all
HOME REGIONAL OFFICES PRESS CENTER ABOUT ADL CONTACT US
ADL
Anti-Defamation League
CONTRIBUTE
TRIBUTE E-CARDS
Get ADL's online newsletters:
SUBSCRIBE
UPDATE YOUR PROFILE
Education
E-Mail This to A Friend
Religion in the Public Schools
Introduction
The issue of the proper role of religion in the public schools continues to be the subject of great controversy. School officials, parents and students -- as well as lawyers and judges -- wrestle with these questions every day. However, clear standards and guidance are elusive. This handbook will help provide a roadmap through this terrain.
It is important to bear in mind that this issue is extremely complex. Decision makers must address many competing demands, invariably looking to balance the twin constitutional mandates of separation of church and state and the right to freely exercise religion. They must include in their thinking the needs and rights of both the religious and the non-religious. Furthermore, decision makers must strive towards a vision of a pluralistic America that is open and welcoming to all groups, including religious minorities.
Introduction
Background: Religious Liberty in America
Prayer in Public School

APPROVED WEB SITE

Anti-Defamation League

Founded in 1913, the Anti-Defamation League is committed "to secur[ing] justice and fair treatment to all." Explore the role of religion in public education at its Web site.

Access this Web site from http://www.myreportlinks.com

whether the government could provide funding to the District of Columbia, which would, in turn, help finance a hospital that would be built and operated by the Roman Catholic Church.

The Supreme Court determined that even though the District of Columbia was neither a state nor had a legislature, the Commissioners who ran the District served that function. Therefore, they were acting within the scope of their authority in providing the funding. As a result, the Court upheld the grant. The decision was supported by the fact that the land would not be owned by the church and there was nothing openly religious about operating a hospital.[1]

In 1947, the court issued its first decision that explicitly interpreted the establishment clause to mean that there must be a complete separation of church and state.

The State of New Jersey allowed local school boards to pay for the transportation costs of children attending private schools, including Catholic schools. A taxpayer in Ewing Township, Arch R. Everson, sued on the grounds that religion was being directly supported by taxpayer money. And as a taxpayer, Everson did not want his money being used to support any one religion.

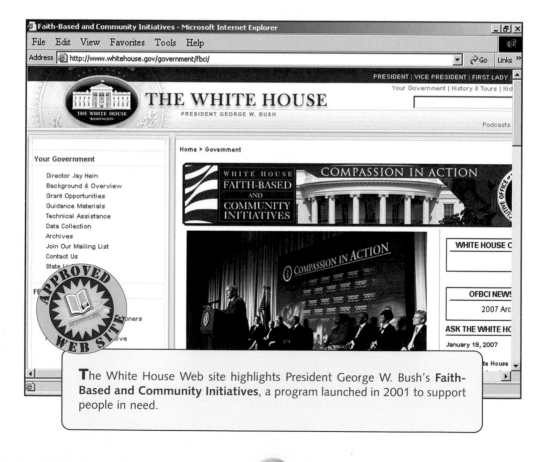

The White House Web site highlights President George W. Bush's **Faith-Based and Community Initiatives**, a program launched in 2001 to support people in need.

In *Everson* v. *Board of Education,* the Supreme Court held that the New Jersey statute was legal. But the court's ruling laid the groundwork for the complete separation of church and state in the future. Justice Hugo Black wrote for the majority:

> The 'establishment of religion' clause of the First Amendment means at least this: Neither a state nor the Federal Government can set up a church. Neither can pass laws which aid one religion, aid all religions or prefer one religion over another. . . . No tax in any amount, large or small, can be levied to support any religious activities or institutions. . . . Neither a state nor the Federal Government can, openly or secretly, participate in the affairs of any religious organizations or groups and vice versa. In the words of Jefferson, the clause against establishment of religion by law was intended to erect 'a wall of separation between Church and State.'[2]

➔ WALL OF SEPARATION

In 1948, the Supreme Court heard *McCollum* v. *Board of Education,* a case that dealt with an Illinois program that allowed public schools to release students from normal classroom instruction in order to receive religious education. The classes were taught inside the school and by instructors provided by various faiths at no cost to the school; however, the school board did retain the right to approve the instructors. Once again, the court invoked the "wall of separation" metaphor to strike down the program.

⊜BRICKS IN THE WALL

The Supreme Court found that the Illinois program clearly violated the First Amendment's requirement that a tax-supported public school cannot help any particular religion at the expense of any other particular religion.[3]

The opinion then states:

> . . . [The] First Amendment rests upon the premise that both religion and government can best work to achieve their lofty aims if each is left free from the other within its respective sphere. Or, as we said in the Everson case, the First Amendment had erected a wall between Church and State which must be kept high and impregnable.[4]

Just four years later, the same Supreme Court upheld a similar student release program in New York City. The difference between the cases being that, in *Zorach* v. *Clauson,* the religious instruction was not conducted on public property. In this instance, students had been transported off school grounds, thus removing the implication that the government was requiring or forcing students to participate in a religious function.

➡FORCED FAITH

The court's ruling in *Zorach* is seen as an example of adapting the law for religion, rather than totally agreeing with the complete separation of church and state.[5] However, the decision did not weigh the possibility that some students might single out other students who did not attend religious instruction off campus. In other words, some non-religious children might feel compelled to participate in some form of religious activity.

➡ *WALZ V. TAX COMMISSION*

Walz v. Tax Commission (1970) illustrates the conflict between an individual's free exercise of religion and a government acting to promote establishment of religion. This case confronted the dilemma of whether charitable organizations, such as churches, should be required to pay property tax.

If the court upheld the exemption, religious organizations would benefit financially because they would not be required to pay property tax. Not paying the tax would represent a huge savings because many churches own a great deal of property. However, if the exemption was struck down, then some religious groups would be heavily burdened by the tax, which would then make it more difficult to practice their religion. The Supreme Court's opinion read, in part:

Appointed to the Supreme Court in 1969 by President Richard Nixon, Chief Justice Warren Burger delivered a variety of important opinions on such issues as abortion, segregation, and the religion clause of the First Amendment.

The course of constitutional neutrality in [matters of religion] cannot be an absolutely straight line; rigidity could well defeat the basic purpose of these provisions, which is to insure that no religion be sponsored or favored, none commanded, and none inhibited.[6]

The Supreme Court decided that the tax exemption created fewer problems than it would if the Supreme Court required taxation. In addition, the Court asserted that the exemption tended to reinforce the desired separation of church and state.

LEMON V. KURTZMAN

In 1971, the Supreme Court reviewed a Pennsylvania state law that allowed school boards to reimburse private schools for teacher salaries and instructional materials. In addition, *Lemon v. Kurtzman* took a fresh look at a Rhode Island law that said state funds could be used to supplement the salaries of private-school instructors. Realizing the difficulty of the entanglements of the First Amendment, Chief Justice Warren Burger wrote:

> The language of the Religion Clauses of the First Amendment is at best opaque [difficult to understand], particularly when compared with other portions of the Amendment. Its authors did not simply prohibit the establishment of a state church or a state religion. . . . Instead they commanded that there should be 'no law respecting an establishment of religion.' A law may be one 'respecting' the forbidden objective while falling short of its total realization.[7]

In other words, a law prohibiting the establishment of a state religion would have made matters clear: it would be illegal for the government to force citizens to adhere to any particular religion. However, the First Amendment is not entirely clear on the matter: there can be no law regarding the establishment of religion. As it is written, the Amendment makes it illegal for the government to interfere with citizens' religious choices.

⊖THE LEMON TEST

Chief Justice Burger devised a test to determine if using state funds to reimburse private-school teachers is, in fact, constitutional, or if it violates the First Amendment. Based on Court rulings over a long period of time, Burger developed a three-part question to determine if a legal action violated the establishment clause of the First Amendment. If a law or ruling passed all three parts, then it could be considered constitutional.

According to Burger's opinion, a law must not have any religious intent, it could not advance or support any religion, and, finally, the law could not do anything to advance "an excessive government entanglement with religion."[8]

Justice Burger's three-pronged test has become known as the "Lemon test," and is still used today when analyzing the legality of a statute. Utilizing this test, the Supreme Court found that both the Pennsylvania and Rhode Island laws violated the First Amendment and were therefore unconstitutional.

→SCHOOL PRAYER

In addition to whether or not religious organizations should benefit from either direct or indirect government funding, there is the question of how readily government should support religious activity. One of the most prominent battlegrounds has been the issue of school prayer. If prayer in school is sanctioned, or allowed, is the government, in effect, supporting the establishment of religion or religious ideas? Or is school prayer simply an acceptable accommodation to religious belief and therefore not in opposition to the separation of church and state?

➔ *ENGEL V. VITALE*

The first case to examine the issue, *Engel v. Vitale,* was brought before the Supreme Court in 1962. At the time, the State of New York opened each school day with the following prayer written by school officials: "Almighty God, we acknowledge our dependence upon Thee, and we beg Thy blessings upon us, our parents, our teachers and our country. Amen." Time was set aside to recite the prayer every morning, but students were not required to recite it.

The U.S. Supreme Court under Chief Justice Earl Warren found that government-directed prayer in public schools was unconstitutional. The court ruled that a vaguely worded prayer written by government officials is a religious act and one that violated the First Amendment's establishment clause. The fact that participation was voluntary made no difference. Justice Hugo Black wrote in the majority opinion:

> We think that the constitutional prohibition against laws respecting an establishment of religion must at least mean that in this country it is no part of the business of government to compose official prayers for any group of the American

Earl Warren was chief justice of the Supreme Court from 1953 until 1969 and widely considered one of the most influential justices in American history. In 1962, he delivered the opinion that found government-directed school prayer unconstitutional.

people to recite as a part of a religious program carried on by government.[9]

→ PRAYER OR MEDITATION

In 1963, the Supreme Court went even further when it declared that reading the Bible in public schools violated the establishment clause of the First Amendment. With *Abington Township School District* v. *Schempp,* the Court held that

> [t]hese exercises are prescribed as part of the curricular activities of students who are required by law to attend school. They are held in the school buildings under the supervision and with the participation of teachers employed in those schools. . . . [Given] the religious character of the exercises . . . the exercises and the law requiring them are in violation of the Establishment Clause.[10]

The Supreme Court has noted that even requiring a moment of silence for prayer or meditation in a public school is not allowed. In the 1985 case *Wallace* v. *Jaffree,* the Court struck down an Alabama state law that required just such a moment. The author of the majority opinion, Justice John Paul Stevens wrote:

> Just as the right to speak and the right to refrain from speaking are complementary components of a broader concept of individual freedom of mind, so also the individual's freedom to choose his own creed is the counterpart of his right to refrain from accepting the creed established by the majority.[11]

In other words, the Constitution guarantees Americans freedom of speech and religion, and no one may try to force any particular speech or religion, or lack thereof, upon anyone else.

➡RELIGIOUS DISPLAYS

Are religious displays on government property an unspoken way of establishing religion? Do such displays simply allow people to express their religious beliefs or are they merely set up for the sake of historical tradition? In recent times, the issue of religious displays on government property has been as controversial as the issue of school prayer.

In 1989, the Supreme Court heard *County of Allegheny* v. *ACLU*. The case concerned a nativity scene placed in Pennsylvania County Courthouse and a second display of a menorah on public property. Justice Harry Blackmun wrote, "[t]he government's use of religious symbolism is unconstitutional if it has the effect of endorsing religious beliefs."[12]

The Court disallowed the nativity scene since its placement in the courthouse effectively endorsed religion; however, the Court found the placement of the Menorah was acceptable since it was not located in an open area and was displayed along with other symbols of the winter holiday season.

→FREE EXERCISE OF RELIGION CASES

The free exercise clause (*"Congress shall make no law respecting an establishment of religion, or prohibiting the free exercise thereof. . . ."*) gives Americans the right to believe whatever they want to believe—no exceptions. However, the right to *act on* belief is limited. For example, there are some extreme religious practices that might require human sacrifice. But because the act of taking another human life is illegal, government can regulate and limit such religious actions in the interest of society and the greater good.

The first major case to balance personal religious liberty against the general welfare was *Reynolds* v. *United States,* heard in 1878. George Reynolds was a Mormon convicted of bigamy, or the crime of having two wives at the same time. Reynolds argued that his Mormon faith required him to marry multiple times. The court disagreed, asserting that "Laws are made for the government of actions, and while they cannot interfere with mere religious belief and opinions, they may with practices."[13] However, the courts have interpreted these limitations on religious activity very narrowly.

In 1940, the court heard *Cantwell v. Connecticut,* one of the first cases to impose the First Amendment and the Bill of Rights on the individual states. In the case, the Cantwell family, three

The question of religion and its "proper" role in American society has always been very controversial. Indeed, the establishment clause of the First Amendment has been and continues to be challenged by both supporters and opponents of organized religions.

Jehovah's Witnesses, went door-to-door in a largely Catholic neighborhood in New Haven, Connecticut, trying to recruit new members. As they did so, they played recordings that attacked organized religion and the Roman Catholic Church. The Cantwells were arrested for breach of the peace and for soliciting without a permit.

→SPEAK YOUR MIND

The Court found that the Cantwells' arrest was unconstitutional. The Court declared that the Cantwells had the right to express their religious beliefs in a public place, and that playing a record did not constitute a threat likely to breach the peace. The court reached this decision after weighing the Cantwells' right to express their religious faith against the possible threat to the community.[14]

The modern view of free expression was set by the 1963 case, *Sherbert* v. *Verner.* Adeil Sherbert, a member of the Seventh-day Adventist Church, worked in a textile mill. When her employer demanded that she work six days each week, including Saturday, Sherbert refused. According to her faith, Saturday must be a day of rest. She was fired. Sherbert could not find any other work. She applied for unemployment compensation, but her claim was denied by the Employment Security Commission. Her claim was denied by South Carolina and she appealed to the Supreme Court.

Justice William J. Brennan wrote for the majority. He held that under the free exercise clause, Sherbert could legally decide not to work on Saturdays. If the South Carolina State Supreme Court decided to deny Sherbert's unemployment compensation claim, it would have to prove that it was not violating the free exercise clause. It would also have to show that it had a good reason, such as protecting the well-being of other people, to deny the claim.

The Supreme Court found that South Carolina had not done so and reinstated Sherbert's unemployment benefits. The Court's decision served as the determining factor for government action with respect to the free exercise clause. The Sherbert test was later overtaken by *Employment Division* v. *Smith,* in which the Court found that the state could fire a person for using peyote, an illegal drug, even though the use of the drug was part of a religious ritual. The Court's ruling meant that states might have the power to allow illegal acts in the pursuit of religion, but that states are not required to do so.

5 FREEDOM OF SPEECH

*I*n addition to freedom of religion, the Founding Fathers believed that the freedom to express ideas was a cornerstone of true democracy. This is generally referred to as freedom of speech, though this right includes more than just the spoken and written word. For example, artistic expression through music, art, and dance is protected by the First Amendment's right to free speech.

While Americans are free to believe in or worship whatever they want, the freedom of speech involves action on the part of an individual. However, just as with the free exercise clause, an individual's right of free speech is weighed against the interest of the larger community.

Furthermore, freedom of speech and freedom of the press are rights generally related to the larger freedom of expression. However, there are some important cases relating to the press, which includes television, radio, movies, the Internet, and many other technologies through which Americans get their information and which spread ideas.

➔ SEDITION CASES

The American Revolution was fought in no small part because the colonists believed they should be free to express themselves and free to disagree with government policy. However, once they had achieved their goal and established a new government, many of the Founding Fathers became sensitive to criticisms.

In 1798, Congress, controlled by the Federalist Party, passed the Alien and Sedition Acts, which President John Adams signed into law. These four laws were designed to protect the new American government from criticism and from foreign agents who wanted to weaken the new democracy. The laws made it a crime to publish "false, scandalous, and malicious writing" against the government or its officials. The Acts were similar to the English seditious libel laws that Americans found so unacceptable just twenty years before.

The Alien and Sedition Acts were in direct conflict with the First Amendment and today would be considered unconstitutional. Thomas Jefferson, who took over as president in 1801, was opposed to the acts and eventually allowed them to expire.[1] However, judicial review of

JOHN QUINCY ADAMS.

Sixth President of the United States.

Born July 11th 1767—Inaugurated March 4th 1825—Retired March 4th 1829.—

Died Feb. 23rd 1848.

▲ Though he was a Founding Father and the second president, John Adams passed the Alien and Sedition Acts in 1798, a controversial set of laws that outlawed speech that was critical of America.

Congressional Acts by the United States Supreme Court was established in 1803, when the Court determined that it could overturn a law passed by Congress if that law violated the Constitution. This ruling firmly established the principle of judicial review.

The first major case to address the limits of freedom of speech came in response to the Espionage Act of 1917, which made it illegal to speak out against the United States government or military during World War I. In 1917, Charles Schenck distributed flyers to military draftees urging them not to serve. Schenck hoped to convince enough people to peacefully resist that the

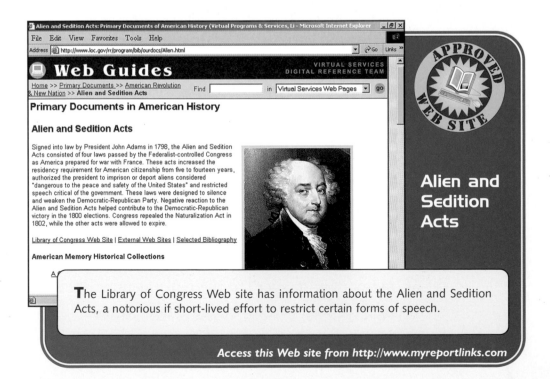

Alien and Sedition Acts: Primary Documents of American History (Virtual Programs & Services, Li - Microsoft Internet Explorer

File   Edit   View   Favorites   Tools   Help

Address http://www.loc.gov/rr/program/bib/ourdocs/Alien.html   Go   Links »

Web Guides   VIRTUAL SERVICES
                                                  DIGITAL REFERENCE TEAM

Home >> Primary Documents >> American Revolution   Find   in Virtual Services Web Pages   go
& New Nation >> Alien and Sedition Acts

Primary Documents in American History

Alien and Sedition Acts

Signed into law by President John Adams in 1798, the Alien and Sedition Acts consisted of four laws passed by the Federalist-controlled Congress as America prepared for war with France. These acts increased the residency requirement for American citizenship from five to fourteen years, authorized the president to imprison or deport aliens considered "dangerous to the peace and safety of the United States" and restricted speech critical of the government. These laws were designed to silence and weaken the Democratic-Republican Party. Negative reaction to the Alien and Sedition Acts helped contribute to the Democratic-Republican victory in the 1800 elections. Congress repealed the Naturalization Act in 1802, while the other acts were allowed to expire.

Library of Congress Web Site | External Web Sites | Selected Bibliography

American Memory Historical Collections

APPROVED WEB SITE

Alien and Sedition Acts

The Library of Congress Web site has information about the Alien and Sedition Acts, a notorious if short-lived effort to restrict certain forms of speech.

Access this Web site from http://www.myreportlinks.com

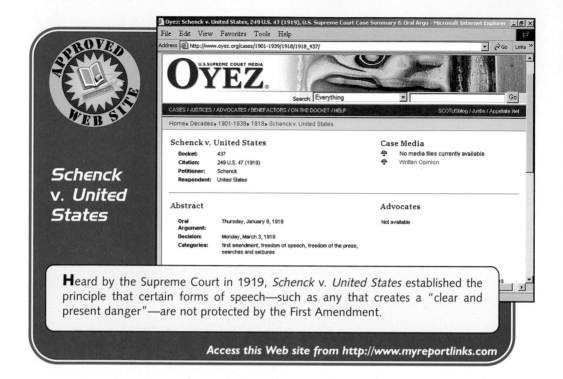

Schenck v. United States

Heard by the Supreme Court in 1919, *Schenck* v. *United States* established the principle that certain forms of speech—such as any that creates a "clear and present danger"—are not protected by the First Amendment.

Access this Web site from http://www.myreportlinks.com

government would have no choice but to repeal the act that authorized the draft. He was arrested for promoting insubordination in the military and obstructing recruitment during a time of war.

The Supreme Court heard *Schenck* v. *United States* in 1919. It ruled that Schenck's criticism of the draft was not protected by the First Amendment. The Court said Schenck's action created a "clear and present danger" to the enlistment and recruiting practices of the United States armed forces during a state of war and thus potentially jeopardized the community.

Justice Oliver Wendell Holmes, Jr., wrote in his majority opinion, "The most stringent protection of free speech would not protect a man in falsely shouting fire in a theatre and causing a panic. It does not even protect a man from an injunction against uttering words that may have all the effect of force."[2]

And further stated:

> The question in every case is whether the words used are used in such circumstances and are of such a nature as to create a clear and present danger that they will bring about the substantive evils that Congress has a right to prevent. . . . It seems to be admitted that if an actual obstruction of the recruiting service were proved, liability for words that produced that effect might be enforced.[3]

A Supreme Court justice from 1902 until 1932, Oliver Wendell Holmes delivered the Court's unanimous 1919 decision that outlawed certain types of speech.

→CLEAR AND PRESENT DANGER

Benjamin Gitlow's case against the State of New York was heard six years after the Schenck case. Though it was not instrumental in expanding the application of the Bill of Rights to laws passed by state governments, it did serve to strengthen Justice Holmes "clear and present danger" requirement. Justice Sanford wrote:

> That utterances inciting to the overthrow of organized government by unlawful means, present a sufficient danger of substantive evil to bring their punishment within the range of legislative discretion, is clear. Such utterances, by their very nature, involve danger to the public peace and to the security of the State . . . [The state] cannot reasonably be required to defer the adoption of measures for its own peace and safety until the revolutionary utterances lead to actual disturbances of the public peace.[4]

Same aspects of the Espionage Act of 1917 and the Sedition Act of 1918 were repealed in 1921. These laws were replaced in 1940 by the Alien Registration Act, commonly known as the Smith Act. It was named for Congressman Howard W. Smith. The Alien Registration Act made it a crime to "knowingly or willfully advocate, abet, advise or teach the duty, necessity, desirability or propriety of overthrowing the Government of the United States or of any State by force or violence, or for anyone to organize any association which teaches, advises

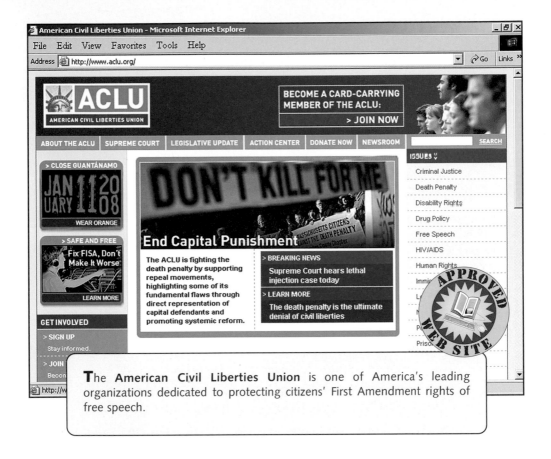

The **American Civil Liberties Union** is one of America's leading organizations dedicated to protecting citizens' First Amendment rights of free speech.

or encourages such an overthrow, or for anyone to become a member of or to affiliate with any such association."[5]

➔ DENNIS V. UNITED STATES

In 1948, Eugene Dennis and several other leaders of the Communist party were arrested under the Smith Act for conspiring to organize as the Communist party and advocating the overthrow of the government of the United States by force. In *Dennis v. United States*, heard in 1950, the Supreme Court found that Dennis's conviction for conspiring to overthrow the United States government did not violate his First Amendment rights. Chief Justice Fred M. Vinson explained in his opinion:

> The doctrine that there must be a clear and present danger of a substantive evil that Congress has a right to prevent is a judicial rule to be applied as a matter of law by the courts. . . . Whether the First Amendment protects the activity which constitutes the violation of the statute must depend upon a judicial determination of the scope of the First Amendment applied to the circumstances of the case.[6]

CRIMINAL BELIEFS

In other words, the Court decided that the government had the right to defend itself from the clear and present danger presented by Communist party activity. "Certainly an attempt to overthrow the Government by force . . . is a sufficient evil for Congress to prevent."[7]

With its findings in *Dennis* v. *United States,* the Court determined that simple belief in an idea was enough for conviction, which is seemingly at odds with the idea that government can't tell you what to think or believe. And while the Court has never explicitly overturned that decision, it has ruled differently in other cases and stated that it is not the belief that can be held as criminal, but acting on that belief.

➜EVIL INTENT

In 1957, the Supreme Court reinterpreted the Smith Act under circumstances almost identical to those in the *Dennis* case. In *Yates* v. *United States,* several Communist party leaders had been arrested under the Smith Act for conspiring to organize as the Communist party and advocating the over-throw of the U.S. government. The Court held that for the Smith Act to be violated, people must advo-cate taking action, not just hold a certain belief. The Court drew a distinction between a statement of an idea and the advocacy that a certain action be taken. Justice John Marshall Harlan wrote:

> We recognize that distinctions between advocacy or teaching of abstract doctrines, with evil intent, and that which is directed to stirring people to action, are often subtle and difficult to grasp, for in a broad sense, as Mr. Justice Holmes said in his dissenting opinion in Gitlow: 'Every idea is an incitement.'[8]

➜KU KLUX KLAN

In 1969, the Supreme Court further expanded the right of free speech by holding that government cannot punish inflammatory speech unless that speech is specifically intended to convince people to break the law.

Clarence Brandenburg was a Ku Klux Klan leader who contacted an Ohio radio station to

NO MORE LIVES!

IMPEACH

Freedom of Speech allows people to say anything they want—as long as their words do not create a dangerous situation. Here people are protesting against the Iraq war and the policies of President George W. Bush.

While offensive to many people, so-called hate speech is protected by the First Amendment. Here, H. W. Evans, then leader of the Ku Klux Klan, a white-supremacist organization, leads a protest in Washington, D.C., in 1926.

discuss a planned march on Washington, D.C. Brandenburg was convicted under an Ohio State law that made it illegal to advocate sabotage or violence as a means of political reform. In a unanimous *per curiam* decision (a statement issued by the Court itself rather than by one justice), the Supreme Court introduced the "imminent lawless action test," which considered one's right to free speech against government interests to protect the peace.

In *Brandenburg v. Ohio*, the court noted that its "decisions have fashioned the principle that the constitutional guarantees of free speech and free press do not permit a State to forbid or proscribe advocacy of the use of force or of law violation except where such advocacy is directed to inciting or producing imminent lawless action."[9]

→ ACTIONS AND WORDS

Flag burning is an example of speech that is defined by actions and not words. By expressing contempt for an American flag, the burner is expressing an idea or concept. This is protected by the First Amendment. In 1989, the court held in *Texas* v. *Johnson* that a Texas statute that criminalized flag burning violated the First Amendment. The Texas law was overturned. Justice William J. Brennan wrote "[t]he First Amendment literally forbids the abridgment only of 'speech,' but we

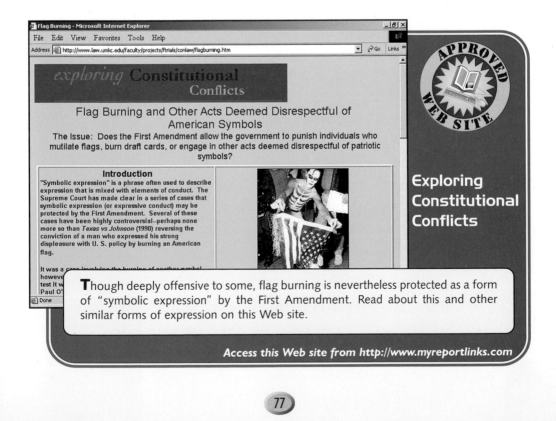

Though deeply offensive to some, flag burning is nevertheless protected as a form of "symbolic expression" by the First Amendment. Read about this and other similar forms of expression on this Web site.

Access this Web site from http://www.myreportlinks.com

have long recognized that its protection does not end at the spoken or written word."[10]

In 1989, Congress passed the Flag Protection Act, which specifically banned flag burning. The Supreme Court promptly struck down the act as unconstitutional, asserting that the government's interest in preserving the flag as a symbol did not outweigh the individual right to disparage that symbol by destroying it. In *United States* v. *Eichman* (1990), which overturned a 1989 law banning the desecration of the flag, Justice Brennan wrote:

> We are aware that desecration of the flag is deeply offensive to many. . . . [But] 'If there is a bedrock principle underlying the First Amendment, it is that the Government may not prohibit the expression of an idea simply because society finds the idea itself offensive or disagreeable.' Punishing desecration of the flag dilutes the very freedom that makes this emblem so revered, and worth revering.[11]

Unpopular and offensive speech has always generated controversy. Some people want to limit what they feel is offensive speech; others push to test the

To many, the American flag and the Bible (shown here) are the two most important symbols of American life. To others, they represent oppression—the beauty of America is that each group can adhere to its own beliefs.

limits of free speech. It has been determined that obscene speech generally has no protection under the First Amendment. But pornography, which also offends many people, is subject to little regulation.

Until 1957, the United States relied on an 1868 English legal case, *Regina* v. *Hicklin,* to define what constituted obscenity under American law. The *Hicklin* test stated that any material that tended to "deprave and corrupt those whose minds are open to such immoral influences, and into whose hands a publication of this sort may fall" was deemed "obscene" and could be banned on that basis.

➔OBSCENITY CASES

Samuel Roth, a New York City bookseller, was convicted under a federal statute for selling obscene and vulgar material through the mail. In *Roth* v. *United States* (1957), the Supreme Court rejected the *Hicklin* test and defined obscenity more strictly: "Whether to the average person, applying contemporary community standards, the dominant theme of the material taken as a whole appeals to prurient [sexual] interest." However, the court's decision reaffirmed the idea that obscenity was not protected by the First Amendment, and upheld Roth's conviction.[12]

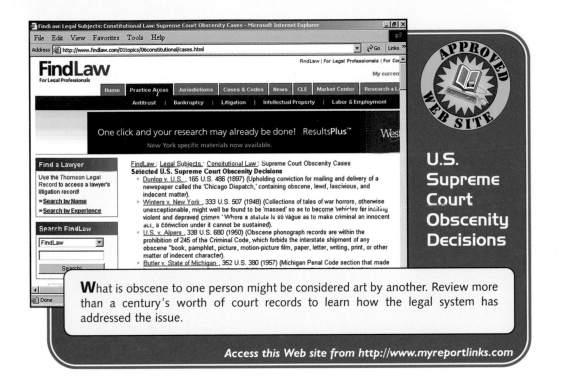

FindLaw: Legal Subjects: Constitutional Law: Supreme Court Obscenity Cases - Microsoft Internet Explorer

File   Edit   View   Favorites   Tools   Help

Address http://www.findlaw.com/01topics/06constitutional/cases.html   Go   Links

FindLaw
For Legal Professionals

FindLaw | For Legal Professionals | For Co

My curren

Home   Practice Areas   Jurisdictions   Cases & Codes   News   CLE   Market Center   Research a L

Antitrust | Bankruptcy | Litigation | Intellectual Property | Labor & Employment

One click and your research may already be done!   ResultsPlus™   West

New York specific materials now available.

Find a Lawyer

Use the Thomson Legal Record to access a lawyer's litigation record!

» Search by Name
» Search by Experience

Search FindLaw

FindLaw

Search!

FindLaw : Legal Subjects : Constitutional Law : Supreme Court Obscenity Cases
Selected U.S. Supreme Court Obscenity Decisions
- Dunlop v. U.S. , 165 U.S. 486 (1897) (Upholding conviction for mailing and delivery of a newspaper called the 'Chicago Dispatch,' containing obscene, lewd, lascivious, and indecent matter).
- Winters v. New York , 333 U.S. 507 (1948) (Collections of tales of war horrors, otherwise unexceptionable, might well be found to be 'massed' so as to become vehicles for inciting violent and depraved crimes 'Where a statute is so vague as to make criminal an innocent act, a conviction under it cannot be sustained).
- U.S. v. Alpers , 338 U.S. 680 (1950) (Obscene phonograph records are within the prohibition of 245 of the Criminal Code, which forbids the interstate shipment of any obscene "book, pamphlet, picture, motion-picture film, paper, letter, writing, print, or other matter of indecent character).
- Butler v. State of Michigan , 352 U.S. 380 (1957) (Michigan Penal Code section that made

Done

**U.S.
Supreme
Court
Obscenity
Decisions**

APPROVED WEB SITE

What is obscene to one person might be considered art by another. Review more than a century's worth of court records to learn how the legal system has addressed the issue.

Access this Web site from http://www.myreportlinks.com

The Court's decision created a problem: How, exactly, is obscenity defined in legal terms? The Supreme Court tried to clarify the matter in 1973 when it heard *Miller* v. *California*. Marvin Miller sold "adult" literature through the mail. He was convicted under a state law that made it a crime to knowingly distribute obscene materials. Chief Justice Burger wrote the majority opinion, first making it clear that "obscene material is not protected by the First Amendment," and then establishing what came to be called the *Miller* Test:

The basic guidelines for the trier of fact must be:
(a) whether 'the average person, applying contemporary community standards' would find that

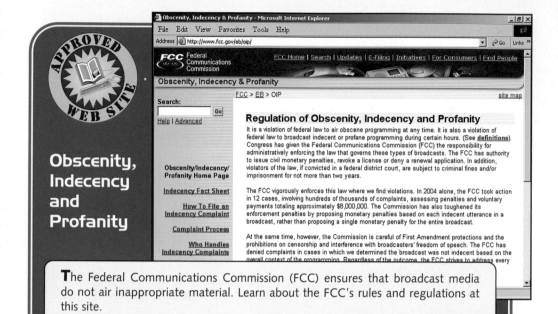

FCC Home | Search | Updates | E-Filing | Initiatives | For Consumers | Find People

Obscenity, Indecency & Profanity

FCC > EB > OIP   site map

Search:

Help | Advanced

Regulation of Obscenity, Indecency and Profanity

It is a violation of federal law to air obscene programming at any time. It is also a violation of
federal law to broadcast indecent or profane programming during certain hours. (See **definitions**).
Congress has given the Federal Communications Commission (FCC) the responsibility for
administratively enforcing the law that governs these types of broadcasts. The FCC has authority
to issue civil monetary penalties, revoke a license or deny a renewal application. In addition,
violators of the law, if convicted in a federal district court, are subject to criminal fines and/or
imprisonment for not more than two years.

The FCC vigorously enforces this law where we find violations. In 2004 alone, the FCC took action
in 12 cases, involving hundreds of thousands of complaints, assessing penalties and voluntary
payments totaling approximately $8,000,000. The Commission has also toughened its
enforcement penalties by proposing monetary penalties based on each indecent utterance in a
broadcast, rather than proposing a single monetary penalty for the entire broadcast.

At the same time, however, the Commission is careful of First Amendment protections and the
prohibitions on censorship and interference with broadcasters' freedom of speech. The FCC has
denied complaints in cases in which we determined the broadcast was not indecent based on the
overall context of the programming. Regardless of the outcome, the FCC strives to address every

Obscenity/Indecency/
Profanity Home Page

Indecency Fact Sheet

How To File an
Indecency Complaint

Complaint Process

Who Handles
Indecency Complaints

Obscenity, Indecency and Profanity

The Federal Communications Commission (FCC) ensures that broadcast media
do not air inappropriate material. Learn about the FCC's rules and regulations at
this site.

Access this Web site from http://www.myreportlinks.com

the work, taken as a whole, appeals to the prurient interest; (b) whether the work depicts or
describes, in a patently offensive way, sexual conduct specifically defined by the applicable state
law; and (c) whether the work, taken as a whole,
lacks serious literary, artistic, political, or scientific
value.[13]

Thus, the Supreme Court upheld Miller's
conviction. Its decision was reinforced a few years
later by *New York* v. *Ferber* (1982). The Court held
that state interests in protecting children permits
laws that prohibit the distribution of images
of sexual performances by minors, even where
content does not meet tests of obscenity.[14]

Thurgood Marshall was the first African American to serve on the Supreme Court. His opinion in the 1969 Stanley v. Georgia case is an important benchmark in establishing an individual's right to privacy.

→RIGHT TO PRIVACY

The Court has held that the distribution of obscene materials can be limited by government action, but private possession of those same materials cannot be criminalized. The 1969 *Stanley v. Georgia* case was pivotal in establishing this right to privacy. It established that the government may not prohibit mere possession of obscene matter because it *might* lead to antisocial conduct nor can the government prevent possession on the grounds that possession is necessary in order to distribute materials to others. Justice Thurgood Marshall wrote:

> [Miller] is asserting the right to read or observe what he pleases . . . in the privacy of his own home. . . . Georgia contends that [he] does not have these rights, that there are certain types of materials that the individual may not read or even possess. Georgia justifies this . . . by arguing that the films in the present case are obscene. But we think that mere categorization of these films as 'obscene' is insufficient justification for such a drastic invasion of personal liberties guaranteed by the First and Fourteenth Amendments . . . If the First Amendment means anything, it means that a State has no business telling a man, sitting alone in his own house, what books he may read or what films he may watch. . . .[15]

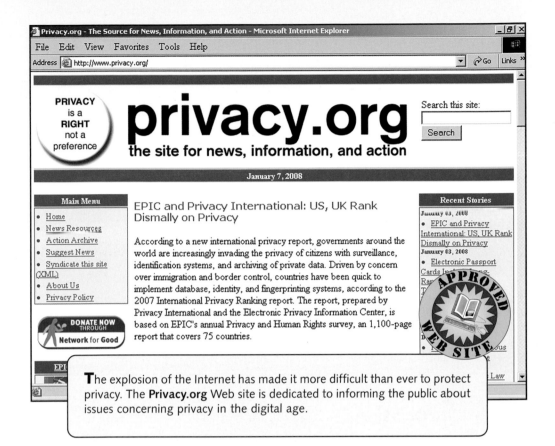

The explosion of the Internet has made it more difficult than ever to protect privacy. The **Privacy.org** Web site is dedicated to informing the public about issues concerning privacy in the digital age.

→ LIBEL AND SLANDER CASES

Libel and slander are forms of defamation, or the communication of false information with the express purpose of harming the reputation of an individual, business, group, product, or government. Libel is a written statement; slander is spoken. Both are intended to mislead people because their false statements are stated or implied to be factual. *New York Times Co.* v. *Sullivan,* which was heard in 1964, set the standard for defamation against public officials.

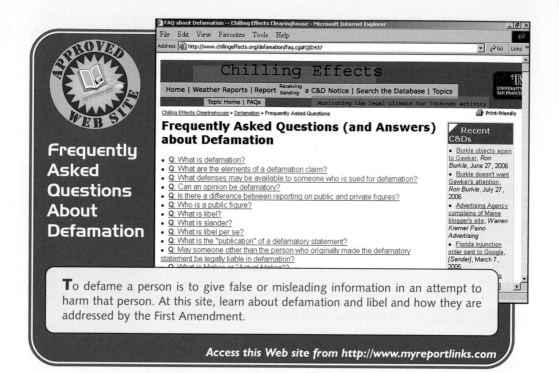

Frequently Asked Questions About Defamation

FAQ about Defamation -- Chilling Effects Clearinghouse - Microsoft Internet Explorer

File   Edit   View   Favorites   Tools   Help

Address http://www.chillingeffects.org/defamation/faq.cgi#QID437

Go   Links »

Chilling Effects

Home | Weather Reports | Report Sending Receiving a C&D Notice | Search the Database | Topics

Topic Home | FAQs

UNIVERSITY SAN FRANCIS

Monitoring the legal climate for Internet activity

Chilling Effects Clearinghouse > Defamation > Frequently Asked Questions

Print-friendly

Frequently Asked Questions (and Answers) about Defamation

- Q: What is defamation?
- Q: What are the elements of a defamation claim?
- Q: What defenses may be available to someone who is sued for defamation?
- Q: Can an opinion be defamatory?
- Q: Is there a difference between reporting on public and private figures?
- Q: Who is a public figure?
- Q: What is libel?
- Q: What is slander?
- Q: What is libel per se?
- Q: What is the "publication" of a defamatory statement?
- Q: May someone other than the person who originally made the defamatory statement be legally liable in defamation?
- Q: What is Malice or "Actual Malice"?

Recent C&Ds

- Burkle objects again to Gawker, *Ron Burkle*, June 27, 2006
- Burkle doesn't want Gawker's attention, *Ron Burkle*, July 27, 2006
- Advertising Agency complains of Maine blogger's site, *Warren Kremer Paino Advertising*
- Florida injunction order sent to Google, *[Sender]*, March 7, 2005

To defame a person is to give false or misleading information in an attempt to harm that person. At this site, learn about defamation and libel and how they are addressed by the First Amendment.

Access this Web site from http://www.myreportlinks.com

On March 29, 1960, *The New York Times* ran a full-page advertisement paid for by supporters of Dr. Martin Luther King, Jr., and others who were working to gain civil rights and racial equality. Though not named in the ad, Police Commissioner L. B. Sullivan of Montgomery, Alabama, argued that the ad contained inaccurate criticisms of the police force in general and him in particular.

The Supreme Court found that *The New York Times* was protected from liability for libel because the statements made in the ad were not made with knowing or reckless disregard for the truth. The Court added that an individual needed to prove that the newspaper had actually tried to hurt him in order for punitive damages to be awarded in a libel case against a newspaper. Justice Brennan wrote:

> The constitutional guarantees require, we think, a federal rule that prohibits a public official from recovering damages for a defamatory falsehood relating to his official conduct unless he proves that the statement was made with 'actual malice'— that is, with knowledge that it was false or with reckless disregard of whether it was false or not.[16]

➔OPINION OR ERROR OF FACT?

In 1974, the Court heard *Gertz* v. *Robert Welch, Inc.,* a case that dealt with the issue of defamation as it related to private individuals.

Elmer Gertz was a lawyer who represented the family of a man who had been shot by the police. The John Birch Society, a conservative political group, printed a story in its newspaper, *American Opinion,* which alleged there was a Communist conspiracy to discredit the police. The article made accusations that Gertz was a Communist, and it included his picture. The Court determined that individual States are free to establish their own standards of liability for defamatory statements made about private individuals. It also determined that opinion cannot be defamatory, or harmful to a person's reputation; only error of fact can be defamatory.

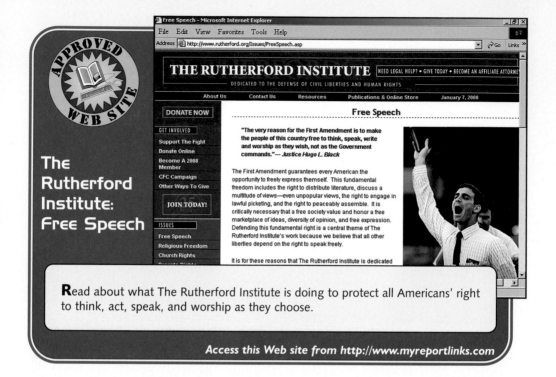

THE RUTHERFORD INSTITUTE

DEDICATED TO THE DEFENSE OF CIVIL LIBERTIES AND HUMAN RIGHTS

Free Speech

"The very reason for the First Amendment is to make the people of this country free to think, speak, write and worship as they wish, not as the Government commands." — *Justice Hugo L. Black*

The First Amendment guarantees every American the opportunity to freely express themself. This fundamental freedom includes the right to distribute literature, discuss a multitude of views—even unpopular views, the right to engage in lawful picketing, and the right to peaceably assemble. It is critically necessary that a free society value and honor a free marketplace of ideas, diversity of opinion, and free expression. Defending this fundamental right is a central theme of The Rutherford Institute's work because we believe that all other liberties depend on the right to speak freely.

It is for these reasons that The Rutherford Institute is dedicated

Read about what The Rutherford Institute is doing to protect all Americans' right to think, act, speak, and worship as they choose.

Access this Web site from http://www.myreportlinks.com

Milkovich v. *Lorain Journal Co.* (1990) has since softened this "error of fact" interpretation by finding that the First Amendment does not allow for a separate "opinion" privilege that limits the application of state defamation laws.

On February 8, 1974, a fight broke out between two rival teams at a wrestling match in Ohio. After a hearing before the Ohio High School Athletic Association (OHSAA), one of the schools was put on probation and suspended from state competition for a year. Several of the school's wrestlers filed suit, arguing that the OHSAA had denied them due process. The court issued a temporary injunction, effectively overruling the OHSAA's decision.

The day after the injunction was granted, a local paper, the *Lorain Journal,* printed a column that implied that one of the coaches, Mike Milkovich, had lied to the court about what happened during the brawl. Milkovich sued the paper. The original trial court issued a directed verdict in favor of the newspaper; however, the Ohio Court of Appeals found for Milkovich, forcing the newspaper to appeal to the Supreme Court. In this instance, the court did not hear the case because it believed there were no significant constitutional issues involved.

⊖Here We Go Again

Over the course of the next few years, the case worked its way through the Ohio legal system again, this time in tandem with another case brought by H. Donald Scott, superintendent of the school system where Milkovich coached. Eventually, Scott's case reached the U.S. Supreme Court, which announced that it would also reconsider the Milkovich decision.

Legal experts expected the Court to strengthen the opinion it issued in the *Gertz* case, when it found that "there is no such thing as a false idea;" in addition, it was expected that the Court would strengthen the idea that a person's opinion is protected from libel. However, the Court argued that it had already established constitutional protection for statements of opinion. Chief Justice William Rehnquist delivered the decision:

> We are not persuaded that, in addition to these protections, an additional separate constitutional privilege for 'opinion' is required to ensure the freedom of expression guaranteed by the First Amendment.[17]

FREEDOM OF THE PRESS

Just as there has been huge debate over the limits of freedom of speech, there has been controversy over the freedom of the press. Censorship and privilege play key roles in this freedom, especially when dealing with modern forms of media.

United States involvement in Southeast Asia and the Vietnam War was an extremely controversial issue in the 1960s and 1970s. When *The New York Times* got hold of a top-secret government study in 1971 that seemed to indicate that American leaders had known for many years that the United States could not win the war, the paper began publishing the document.

The U.S. government, under President Richard Nixon, went to court to stop the *Times* from publishing the document, arguing that the *Times* might irreparably damage the defense interests of the United States. The *Times,* citing its

First Amendment rights, disagreed, igniting a massive battle on the limits of freedom of the press.

New York Times Co. v. *United States* is popularly known as the Pentagon Papers case, because the study of United States involvement in Vietnam commissioned by Secretary of Defense

When Daniel Ellsberg leaked the Pentagon Papers, a confidential study of the Vietnam War, to The New York Times *in 1971, he launched one of the most important First Amendment fights in American history.*

Robert McNamara was coordinated by the Pentagon, which is the headquarters of the Department of Defense. This case has become the primary legal case regarding censorship and "prior restraint," a policy that allows government to legally stop certain documents from being published.

Ultimately, the Supreme Court found that in order to justify prior restraint, the government had to prove that publishing the information would cause "grave and irreparable" danger to the country. In this famous instance, the court felt that the government failed to meet the burden. The *per curiam* decision, notable for how short it was, not only acquitted the *Times,* but ensured that the

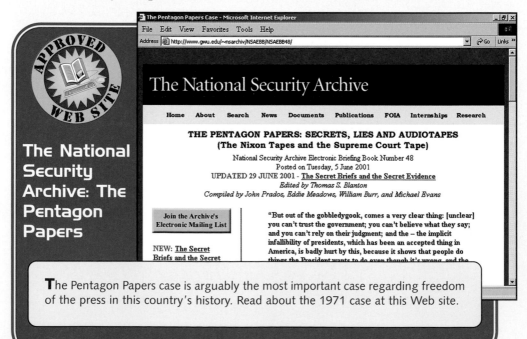

The National Security Archive: The Pentagon Papers

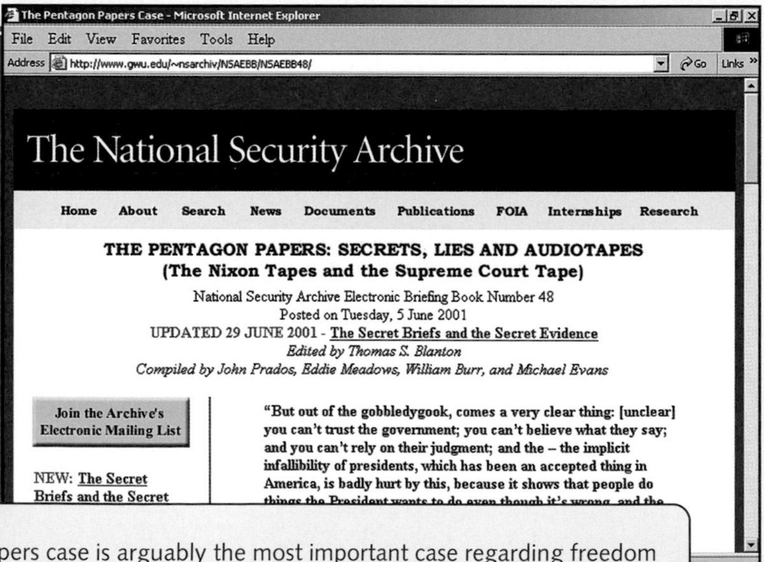
The Pentagon Papers Case - Microsoft Internet Explorer
File Edit View Favorites Tools Help
Address http://www.gwu.edu/~nsarchiv/NSAEBB/NSAEBB48/
The National Security Archive
Home About Search News Documents Publications FOIA Internships Research
THE PENTAGON PAPERS: SECRETS, LIES AND AUDIOTAPES
(The Nixon Tapes and the Supreme Court Tape)
National Security Archive Electronic Briefing Book Number 48
Posted on Tuesday, 5 June 2001
UPDATED 29 JUNE 2001 - The Secret Briefs and the Secret Evidence
Edited by Thomas S. Blanton
Compiled by John Prados, Eddie Meadows, William Burr, and Michael Evans
Join the Archive's Electronic Mailing List
NEW: The Secret Briefs and the Secret
"But out of the gobbledygook, comes a very clear thing: [unclear] you can't trust the government; you can't believe what they say; and you can't rely on their judgment; and the – the implicit infallibility of presidents, which has been an accepted thing in America, is badly hurt by this, because it shows that people do

The Pentagon Papers case is arguably the most important case regarding freedom of the press in this country's history. Read about the 1971 case at this Web site.

Access this Web site from http://www.myreportlinks.com

government would have a tough time in any effort to prevent publication of documents it might wish were secret.

→ LIMITS OF PRESS FREEDOM

The limit of freedom of the press has also been tested in cases where reporters have been called to testify about illegal activities they witnessed.

In 1969, Paul Branzburg, a reporter for *The (Louisville) Courier-Journal,* wrote a story in which he described watching people process and use hashish, an illegal drug. In 1970, Earl Caldwell of *The New York Times* conducted long interviews with members of the Black Panther Party, a radical political group. Paul Pappas, a TV reporter in Massachusetts, also spent several hours in 1970 with the Black Panthers.

In each case, the reporter was called to testify before a grand jury about any illegal activities he might have witnessed. In each case, the reporter refused, citing freedom of the press and the importance of not revealing the identity of a source as the reason why he would not provide the information.

In 1972, the Supreme Court issued a fiercely debated split decision, voting 5-to-4, that stated that the First Amendment granted no such privilege to the press.

→Not So Fast, Reporter

In *Branzburg* v. *Hayes,* Justice Byron White wrote for the majority:

> We do not question the significance of free speech, press, or assembly to the country's welfare. Nor is it suggested that news gathering does not qualify for First Amendment protection. . . . But these cases involve no intrusions upon speech or assembly, no prior restraint or restriction on what the press may publish, and no express or implied command that the press publish what it prefers to withhold. . . .
>
> The sole issue before us is the obligation of reporters to respond to grand jury subpoenas as other citizens do and to answer questions relevant to an investigation into the commission of crime. Citizens generally are not constitutionally immune from grand jury subpoenas. . . .[18]

While the finding in *Branzburg* was seen by some as an attack on freedom of the press, in 1974 the Supreme Court upheld a decision that affirmed that very principle. In *Miami Herald Publishing Co.* v. *Tornillo,* the Court overturned a Florida law that required a newspaper to allow equal access to political candidates in the case of a political editorial or endorsement content. Chief Justice Burger wrote:

> . . . The choice of material to go into a newspaper, and . . . treatment of public issues and public officials—whether fair or unfair—constitute the exercise of editorial control and judgment. It has

yet to be demonstrated how governmental regulation of this crucial process can be exercised consistent with First Amendment guarantees of a free press. . . .[19]

Freedom of expression is a basic American right. Even though the First Amendment is written simply, over time, courts have changed their interpretation of its meaning. From time to time, the cases involved freedom of speech, other times, freedom of religion, and still others related to freedom of the press. Different courts at different times in history have not always agreed. In this way, the U.S. Constitution is always changing.

6 THE CONSTITUTION EVOLVES

*T*he U.S. Constitution is often described as a document that "lives and breathes." In other words, like a man who continues to grow and change, the Constitution changes as the people who interpret it—our elected officials and the Supreme Court—change. And as a result, many of the issues surrounding the interpretation of the First Amendment and the rights it guarantees are constantly being challenged.

➔RELIGION AND SCHOOLS

Like the whole First Amendment, the establishment clause is deceptively simple: *"Congress shall make no law respecting an establishment of religion."* However, the issue becomes complicated when people begin to debate what, exactly, constitutes acceptable governmental support of religion versus what is unacceptable.

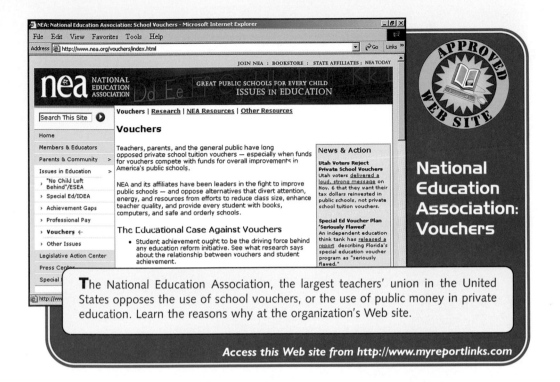

The National Education Association, the largest teachers' union in the United States opposes the use of school vouchers, or the use of public money in private education. Learn the reasons why at the organization's Web site.

Access this Web site from http://www.myreportlinks.com

In 2002, a divided Supreme Court upheld an Ohio law that allowed a public school district in Cleveland to issue school vouchers, or financial credits, which parents could apply toward tuition at private schools, the majority of which had a religious affiliation. The court's decision in *Zelman* v. *Simmons-Harris* removed any constitutional barriers to similar voucher plans in the future. From that time on, public schools could offer vouchers that could be applied to private—even religious— schools. The decision angered people who believe that school vouchers blur Jefferson's famous wall separating church and state.

▲ *Thomas Jefferson believed that religion was a private matter and that government should play no role in supporting it. In 1802, he wrote a letter in which he called for "a wall of separation between church and state."*

In *Zelman,* the Court developed a five-pronged test to determine whether a school voucher program is constitutional. According to the court, if a program can show that it has a valid secular (non-religious) purpose, that the aid goes to parents and not schools, that a broad class of beneficiaries is covered, that the program is neutral with respect to religion, and, finally, that there are adequate nonreligious options, then it is constitutional. Chief Justice Rehnquist found:

> In sum, the Ohio program is entirely neutral with respect to religion. It provides benefits directly to a

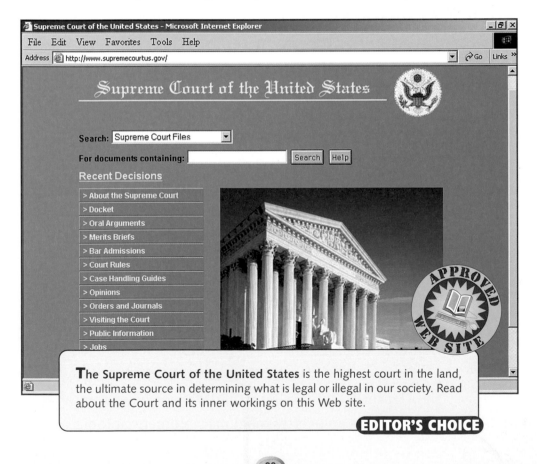

The Supreme Court of the United States is the highest court in the land, the ultimate source in determining what is legal or illegal in our society. Read about the Court and its inner workings on this Web site.

EDITOR'S CHOICE

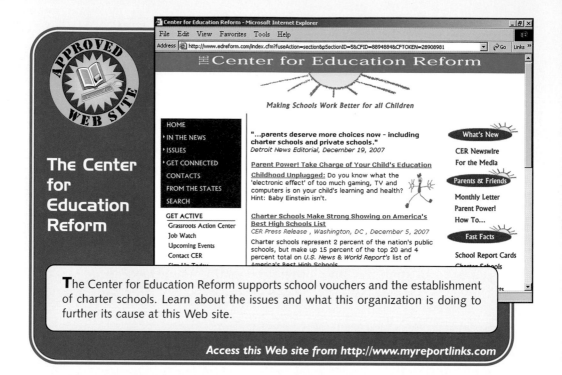

Access this Web site from http://www.myreportlinks.com

wide spectrum of individuals, defined only by financial need and residence in a particular school district. It permits such individuals to exercise genuine choice among options public and private, secular and religious . . . [W]e hold that the program does not offend the Establishment Clause.[1]

The issue of prayer in school—Who can pray? When can they pray? Where can they pray? Is it okay for *anyone* to pray anywhere on school property?—was revisited in 1992 when the Supreme Court heard *Lee* v. *Weisman*.

Mr. and Mrs. Daniel Weisman objected when they learned that a rabbi would deliver what they believed was an overtly religious statement at their daughter's high school graduation in Providence, Rhode Island. They sought a restraining order that would prevent the rabbi from participating. The Rhode Island district court denied their claim.

The Weismans carried their case to the Supreme Court, which found that a prayer during a public school event such as a graduation violated the establishment clause of the First Amendment. Justice Anthony Kennedy wrote:

> We do not hold that every state action implicating religion is invalid if one or a few citizens find it offensive. . . . The prayer exercises in this case are especially improper because the State has in every practical sense compelled attendance and participation in an explicit religious exercise at an event of singular importance to every student, one the objecting student had no real alternative to avoid.[2]

In other words, the prayer was deemed unconstitutional because the student was required to attend the ceremony. The Supreme Court determined that it was illegal for the school district to force religion upon anyone in such a manner.

➔VOLUNTARY PRAYER?

In *Lee v. Weisman,* the Court held that injecting religion into a function that a student was required to attend was unconstitutional. In *Santa Fe Independent School District v. Doe,* heard in 2000, it found that even student-initiated prayer at a voluntary event violated the establishment clause. Justice John Paul Stevens explained, "Even if we regard every high school student's decision to attend a home football game as purely voluntary, we are nevertheless persuaded that the delivery of a pregame prayer has the improper effect of coercing those present to participate in an act of religious worship."[3]

➡RELIGIOUS DISPLAYS ON PUBLIC PROPERTY

In recent years, the Supreme Court has expanded its interpretation of the establishment clause to include religious displays on public property. In 2005, the Supreme Court took on *Van Orden v. Perry,* a case that dealt with the placement of a monument to the Old Testament's Ten Commandments on the grounds of the Texas State Capitol. The Court found that the monument did not violate the establishment clause because, it said, the statue conveyed a historic and social meaning, and did not constitute an intrusive religious endorsement.[4]

This decision stood in contrast to the finding in another case concerning a similar religious display heard at nearly the same time. In *McCreary County v. ACLU of Kentucky,* the Court ruled that displaying the Ten Commandments is an overt religious statement unless its display goes hand-in-hand with a non-religious message. The Court found

The Web site **Ben's Guide to U.S. Government for Kids** has a wealth of information about our country and its history, including the texts of the Constitution and the Bill of Rights.

EDITOR'S CHOICE

that McCreary County made no effort to draw a historical connection between the Ten Commandments and the other documents displayed with it; thus, the display violated the establishment clause of the First Amendment.[5]

Objections to religion intruding on the public have only grown more intense over time. At almost the same time, the public has grown more concerned about pornography, something some people think has become all-too common in society. As a consequence, society in general and the

Supreme Court in particular has struggled with some of the most basic questions relating to it: What is pornography? At what point does something that is acceptable to one person become unacceptable to the public?

→ CHILD PORNOGRAPHY

In *Ashcroft v. Free Speech Coalition,* considered in 2002, the Court struck down two provisions of the Child Pornography Prevention Act of 1996 as being too broad. The first part of the statute that was struck down would have prohibited "any visual depiction, including any photograph, film, video, picture, or computer or computer-generated image or picture" that "is, or appears to be, of a minor engaging in sexually explicit conduct." Justice Anthony Kennedy expressed the Court's view:

> The sexual abuse of a child is a most serious crime and an act repugnant to the moral instincts of a decent people. In its legislative findings, Congress recognized that there are subcultures of persons who harbor illicit desires for children and commit criminal acts to gratify the impulses. . . .
> Congress may pass valid laws to protect children from abuse, and it has. The prospect of crime, however, by itself does not justify laws suppressing protected speech.[6]

Justice Kennedy also pointed out that many critically acclaimed and important literary and

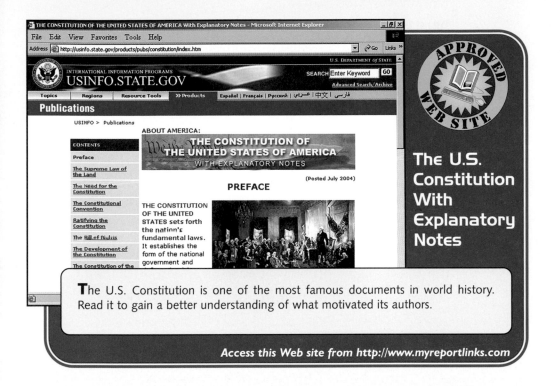

THE CONSTITUTION OF THE UNITED STATES OF AMERICA With Explanatory Notes - Microsoft Internet Explorer

File   Edit   View   Favorites   Tools   Help

Address http://usinfo.state.gov/products/pubs/constitution/index.htm   Go   Links »

U.S. DEPARTMENT of STATE

INTERNATIONAL INFORMATION PROGRAMS
USINFO.STATE.GOV

SEARCH Enter Keyword   GO
Advanced Search/Archive

Topics   Regions   Resource Tools   >> Products   Español | Français | Русский | عـربي | 中文 | فارسی

Publications

USINFO > Publications

ABOUT AMERICA:
THE CONSTITUTION OF
THE UNITED STATES OF AMERICA
WITH EXPLANATORY NOTES

(Posted July 2004)

PREFACE

CONTENTS

Preface

The Supreme Law of
the Land

The Need for the
Constitution

The Constitutional
Convention

Ratifying the
Constitution

The Bill of Rights

The Development of
the Constitution

The Constitution of the

THE CONSTITUTION
OF THE UNITED
STATES sets forth
the nation's
fundamental laws.
It establishes the
form of the national
government and

The U.S.
Constitution
With
Explanatory
Notes

The U.S. Constitution is one of the most famous documents in world history. Read it to gain a better understanding of what motivated its authors.

Access this Web site from http://www.myreportlinks.com

artistic works, like the Academy Award-winning movie *Traffic* and William Shakespeare's *Romeo and Juliet,* would be illegal according to these statutes.

In May 2008, the Supreme Court upheld a 2003 law that had been adopted in an effort to address the Court's earlier concerns. This new law was "a carefully crafted attempt to eliminate the First Amendment problems we identified [in the 2002 decision]," said Justice Anthony Scalia.[7]

➔ BARTNICKI V. VOPPER

The limits of press freedom are also under seemingly constant review. For example, when radio host Frederick Vopper played a tape of a woman named Gloria Bartnicki making threats against members of the local school board, Bartnicki sued Vopper. She claimed that since Vopper knew the recording he had was obtained illegally, playing it on the air was illegal as well.

The Supreme Court heard *Bartnicki* v. *Vopper* in 2001 and found that Vopper could not be held liable. Public safety—the well-being of school-board members—was deemed more important than Bartnicki's privacy. Justice John Paul Stevens stated in the majority opinion:

The **First Amendment Center** works to preserve and protect First Amendment freedoms. Its Web site provides news, analysis, and commentary on the freedoms embodied by the Amendment.

EDITOR'S CHOICE

It seems to us that there are important interests to be considered on *both* sides . . . [W]e acknowledge that some intrusions on privacy are more offensive than others, and that the disclosure of the contents of a private conversation can be an even greater intrusion on privacy than the interception itself. As a result, there is a valid independent justification for prohibiting such disclosures by persons who lawfully obtained access to the contents of an illegally intercepted message. . . .

We think . . . that a stranger's illegal conduct does not suffice to remove the First Amendment shield from speech about a matter of public concern.[8]

THE BOY SCOUTS OF AMERICA

Even the First Amendment right of free association has been challenged in recent years. In *Boy Scouts of America v. Dale,* (2000), the Supreme Court relied on the First Amendment's right of free association to find that a private organization is allowed to exclude a person from membership.

The Boy Scouts of America is a private, not-for-profit organization that tries to instill its system of values in young people. In this case, the Boy Scouts asserted that James Dale, an assistant scoutmaster in New Jersey who was also homosexual, was not an appropriate representative of the group's values. The Boy Scouts revoked his membership when it discovered his sexual preference. Chief Justice Rehnquist wrote:

[E], even if the Boy Scouts discourages Scout leaders from disseminating views on sexual issues . . . the First Amendment protects the Boy Scouts' method of expression. If the Boy Scouts wishes Scout leaders to avoid questions of sexuality and teach only by example, this fact does not negate the sincerity of its belief discussed above. . . ."[9]

The First Amendment gives Americans the freedom to say, believe, and express almost anything we choose—no matter how offensive to others.

The Constitution of the United States

The text of the Constitution is presented here. Most words are given their modern spelling and capitalization. Brackets [ ] indicate parts that have been changed or set aside by amendments.

Preamble

We the People of the United States, in Order to form a more perfect Union, establish Justice, insure domestic Tranquillity, provide for the common defence, promote the general Welfare, and secure the Blessings of Liberty to ourselves and our Posterity, do ordain and establish this Constitution for the United States of America.

Article I
The Legislative Branch

Section 1. All legislative powers herein granted shall be vested in a Congress of the United States, which shall consist of a Senate and House of Representatives.

The House of Representatives

Section 2. The House of Representatives shall be composed of members chosen every second year by the people of the several states, and the electors in each state shall have the qualifications requisite for electors of the most numerous branch of the state legislature.

No person shall be a Representative who shall not have attained to the age of twenty five years, and been seven years a citizen of the United States, and who shall not, when elected, be an inhabitant of that state in which he shall be chosen.

Representatives and direct taxes shall be apportioned among the several states which may be included within this union, according to their respective numbers, [which shall be determined by adding to the whole number of free persons, including those bound to service for a term of years, and excluding Indians not taxed, three fifths of all other persons]. The actual Enumeration shall be made within three years after the first meeting of the Congress of the United States, and within every subsequent term of ten years, in such manner as they shall by law direct. The number of Representatives shall not exceed one for every thirty thousand, but each state shall have at least one Representative; [and until such enumeration shall be made, the state of New Hampshire shall be entitled to chuse three, Massachusetts eight, Rhode Island and Providence Plantations one, Connecticut five, New York six, New Jersey four, Pennsylvania eight, Delaware one, Maryland six, Virginia ten, North Carolina five, South Carolina five, and Georgia three].

When vacancies happen in the Representation from any state, the executive authority thereof shall issue writs of election to fill such vacancies.

The House of Representatives shall choose their speaker and other officers; and shall have the sole power of impeachment.

The Senate

Section 3. The Senate of the United States shall be composed of two Senators from each state, [chosen by the legislature thereof,] for six years; and each Senator shall have one vote.

Immediately after they shall be assembled in consequence of the first election, they shall be divided as equally as may be into three classes. The seats of the Senators of the first class shall be vacated at the expiration of the second year, of the second class at the expiration of the fourth year, and the third class at the expiration of the sixth year, so that one third may be chosen every second year; [and if vacancies happen by resignation, or otherwise, during the recess of the legislature of any state, the executive thereof may make temporary appointments until the next meeting of the legislature, which shall then fill such vacancies].

No person shall be a Senator who shall not have attained to the age of thirty years, and been nine years a citizen of the United States and who shall not, when elected, be an inhabitant of that state for which he shall be chosen.

The Vice President of the United States shall be President of the Senate, but shall have no vote, unless they be equally divided.

The Senate shall choose their other officers, and also a President pro tempore, in the absence of the Vice President, or when he shall exercise the office of President of the United States.

The Senate shall have the sole power to try all impeachments. When sitting for that purpose, they shall be on oath or affirmation. When the President of the United States is tried, the Chief Justice shall preside: And no person shall be convicted without the concurrence of two thirds of the members present.

Judgment in cases of impeachment shall not extend further than to removal from office, and disqualification to hold and enjoy any office of honor, trust or profit under the United States: but the party convicted shall nevertheless be liable and subject to indictment, trial, judgment and punishment, according to law.

Organization of Congress

Section 4. The times, places and manner of holding elections for Senators and Representatives, shall be prescribed in each state by the legislature thereof; but the Congress may at any time by law make or alter such regulations, [except as to the places of choosing senators].

The Congress shall assemble at least once in every year, [and such meeting shall be on the first Monday in December], unless they shall by law appoint a different day.

Section 5. Each House shall be the judge of the elections, returns and qualifications of its own members, and a majority of each shall constitute a quorum to do business; but a smaller number may adjourn from day to day, and may be authorized to compel the attendance of absent members, in such manner, and under such penalties as each House may provide.

Each House may determine the rules of its proceedings, punish its members for disorderly behavior, and, with the concurrence of two thirds, expel a member.

Each House shall keep a journal of its proceedings, and from time to time publish the same, excepting such parts as may in their judgment require secrecy; and the yeas and nays of the members of either House on any question shall, at the desire of one fifth of those present, be entered on the journal.

Neither House, during the session of Congress, shall, without the consent of the other, adjourn for more than three days, nor to any other place than that in which the two Houses shall be sitting.

Section 6. The Senators and Representatives shall receive a compensation for their services, to be ascertained by law, and paid out of the treasury of the United States. They shall in all cases, except treason, felony and breach of the peace, be privileged from arrest during their attendance at the session of their respective Houses, and in going to and returning from the same; and for any speech or debate in either House, they shall not be questioned in any other place.

No Senator or Representative shall, during the time for which he was elected, be appointed to any civil office under the authority of the United States, which shall have been created, or the emoluments whereof shall have been increased during such time: and no person holding any office under the United States, shall be a member of either House during his continuance in office.

Section 7. All bills for raising revenue shall originate in the House of Representatives; but the Senate may propose or concur with amendments as on other Bills.

Every bill which shall have passed the House of Representatives and the Senate, shall, before it become a law, be presented to the President of the United States; if he approve he shall sign it, but if not he shall return it, with his objections to that House in which it shall have originated, who shall enter the objections at large on their journal, and proceed to reconsider it. If after such reconsideration two thirds of that House shall agree to pass the bill, it shall be sent, together with the objections, to the other House, by which it shall likewise be reconsidered, and if approved by two thirds of that House, it shall become a law. But in all such cases the votes of both Houses shall be determined by yeas and nays, and the names of the persons voting for and against the bill shall be entered on the journal of each House respectively. If any bill shall not be returned by the President within ten days (Sundays excepted) after it shall have been presented to him, the same shall be a law, in like manner as if he had signed it, unless the Congress by their adjournment prevent its return, in which case it shall not be a law.

Every order, resolution, or vote to which the concurrence of the Senate and House of Representatives may be necessary (except on a question of adjournment) shall be presented to the President of the United States; and before the same shall take effect, shall be approved by him, or being disapproved by him, shall be repassed by two thirds of the Senate and House of Representatives, according to the rules and limitations prescribed in the case of a bill.

Powers Granted to Congress
The Congress shall have the power:

Section 8. To lay and collect taxes, duties, imposts and excises, to pay the debts and provide for the common defense and general welfare of the United States; but all duties, imposts and excises shall be uniform throughout the United States;

To borrow money on the credit of the United States;

To regulate commerce with foreign nations, and among the several states, and with the Indian tribes;

To establish a uniform rule of naturalization, and uniform laws on the subject of bankruptcies throughout the United States;

To coin money, regulate the value thereof, and of foreign coin, and fix the standard of weights and measures;

To provide for the punishment of counterfeiting the securities and current coin of the United States;

To establish post offices and post roads;

To promote the progress of science and useful arts, by securing for limited times to authors and inventors the exclusive right to their respective writings and discoveries;

To constitute tribunals inferior to the Supreme Court;

To define and punish piracies and felonies committed on the high seas, and offenses against the law of nations;

To declare war, grant letters of marque and reprisal, and make rules concerning captures on land and water;

To raise and support armies, but no appropriation of money to that use shall be for a longer term than two years;

To provide and maintain a navy;

To make rules for the government and regulation of the land and naval forces;

To provide for calling forth the militia to execute the laws of the union, suppress insurrections and repel invasions;

To provide for organizing, arming, and disciplining, the militia, and for governing such part of them as may be employed in the service of the United States, reserving to the states respectively, the appointment of the officers, and the authority of training the militia according to the discipline prescribed by Congress;

To exercise exclusive legislation in all cases whatsoever, over such District (not exceeding ten miles square) as may, by cession of particular states, and the acceptance of Congress, become the seat of the government of the United States, and to exercise like authority over all places purchased by the consent of the legislature of the state in which the same shall be, for the erection of forts, magazines, arsenals, dockyards, and other needful buildings;—And

To make all laws which shall be necessary and proper for carrying into execution the foregoing powers, and all other powers vested by this Constitution in the government of the United States, or in any department or officer thereof.

Powers Forbidden to Congress

Section 9. The migration or importation of such persons as any of the states now existing shall think proper to admit, shall not be prohibited by the Congress prior to the year one thousand eight hundred and eight, but a tax or duty may be imposed on such importation, not exceeding ten dollars for each person.

The privilege of the writ of habeas corpus shall not be suspended, unless when in cases of rebellion or invasion the public safety may require it.

No bill of attainder or ex post facto law shall be passed.

No capitation, [or other direct,] tax shall be laid, unless in proportion to the census or enumeration herein before directed to be taken.

No tax or duty shall be laid on articles exported from any state.

No preference shall be given by any regulation of commerce or revenue to the ports of one state over those of another: nor shall vessels bound to, or from, one state, be obliged to enter, clear or pay duties in another.

No money shall be drawn from the treasury, but in consequence of appropriations made by law; and a regular statement and account of receipts and expenditures of all public money shall be published from time to time.

No title of nobility shall be granted by the United States: and no person holding any office of profit or trust under them, shall, without the consent of the Congress, accept of any present, emolument, office, or title, of any kind whatever, from any king, prince, or foreign state.

Powers Forbidden to the States

Section 10. No state shall enter into any treaty, alliance, or confederation; grant letters of marque and reprisal; coin money; emit bills of credit; make anything but gold and silver coin a tender in payment of debts; pass any bill of attainder, ex post facto law, or law impairing the obligation of contracts, or grant any title of nobility.

No state shall, without the consent of the Congress, lay any imposts or duties on imports or exports, except what may be absolutely necessary for executing its inspection laws: and the net produce of all duties and imposts, laid by any state on imports or exports, shall be for the use of the treasury of the United States; and all such laws shall be subject to the revision and control of the Congress.

No state shall, without the consent of Congress, lay any duty of tonnage, keep troops, or ships of war in time of peace, enter into any agreement or compact with another state, or with a foreign power, or engage in war, unless actually invaded, or in such imminent danger as will not admit of delay.

Article II
The Executive Branch

Section 1. The executive power shall be vested in a President of the United States of America. He shall hold his office during the term of four years, and, together with the Vice President, chosen for the same term, be elected, as follows:

Each state shall appoint, in such manner as the legislature thereof may direct, a number of electors, equal to the whole number of Senators and Representatives to which the State may be entitled in the Congress: but no Senator or Representative, or person holding an office of trust or profit under the United States, shall be appointed an elector.

[The electors shall meet in their respective states, and vote by ballot for two persons, of whom one at least shall not be an inhabitant of the same state with themselves. And they shall make a list of all the persons voted for, and of the number of votes for each; which list they shall sign and certify, and transmit sealed to the seat of the government of the United States, directed to the President of the Senate. The President of the Senate shall, in the presence of the Senate and House of Representatives, open all the certificates, and the votes shall then be counted. The person having the greatest number of votes shall be the President, if such number be a majority of the whole number of electors appointed; and if there be more than one who have such majority, and have an equal number of votes, then the House of Representatives shall immediately choose by ballot one of them for President; and if no person have a majority, then from the five highest on the list the said House shall in like manner choose the President. But in choosing the President, the votes shall be taken by States, the representation from each state having one vote; A quorum for this purpose shall consist of a member or members from two thirds of the states, and a majority of all the states shall be necessary to a choice. In every case, after the choice of the President, the person having the greatest number of votes of the electors shall be the Vice President. But if there should remain two or more who have equal votes, the Senate shall choose from them by ballot the Vice President.]

The Congress may determine the time of choosing the electors, and the day on which they shall give their votes; which day shall be the same throughout the United States.

No person except a natural born citizen, or a citizen of the United States, at the time of the adoption of this Constitution, shall be eligible to the office of President; neither shall any person be eligible to that office who shall not have attained to the age of thirty-five years, and been fourteen Years a resident within the United States.

In case of the removal of the President from office, or of his death, resignation, or inability to discharge the powers and duties of the said office, the same shall devolve on the Vice President, and the Congress may by law provide for the case of removal, death, resignation or inability, both of the President and Vice President, declaring what officer shall then act as President, and such officer shall act accordingly, until the disability be removed, or a President shall be elected.

The President shall, at stated times, receive for his services, a compensation, which shall neither be increased nor diminished during the period for which he shall have been elected, and he shall not receive within that period any other emolument from the United States, or any of them.

Before he enter on the execution of his office, he shall take the following oath or affirmation:—"I do solemnly swear (or affirm) that I will faithfully execute the office of President of the United States, and will to the best of my ability, preserve, protect and defend the Constitution of the United States."

Section 2. The President shall be commander-in-chief of the Army and Navy of the United States, and of the militia of the several states, when called into the actual service of the United States; he may require the opinion, in writing, of the principal officer in each of the executive departments, upon any subject relating to the duties of their respective offices, and he shall have power to grant reprieves and pardons for offenses against the United States, except in cases of impeachment.

He shall have power, by and with the advice and consent of the Senate, to make treaties, provided two-thirds of the Senators present concur; and he shall nominate, and by and with the advice and consent of the Senate, shall appoint ambassadors, other public ministers and consuls, judges of the Supreme Court, and all other officers of the United States, whose appointments are not herein otherwise provided for, and which shall be established by law: but the Congress may by law vest the appointment of such inferior officers, as they think proper, in the President alone, in the courts of law, or in the heads of departments.

The President shall have power to fill up all vacancies that may happen during the recess of the Senate, by granting commissions which shall expire at the end of their next session.

Section 3. He shall from time to time give to the Congress information of the state of the union, and recommend to their consideration such measures as he shall judge necessary and expedient; he may, on extraordinary occasions, convene both Houses, or either of them, and in case of disagreement between them, with respect to the time of adjournment, he may adjourn them to such time as he shall think proper; he shall receive ambassadors and other public ministers; he shall take care that the laws be faithfully executed, and shall commission all the officers of the United States.

Section 4. The President, Vice President and all civil officers of the United States, shall be removed from office on impeachment for, and conviction of, treason, bribery, or other high crimes and misdemeanors.

Article III
The Judicial Branch

Section 1. The judicial power of the United States, shall be vested in one Supreme Court, and in such inferior courts as the Congress may from time to time ordain and establish. The judges, both of the supreme and inferior courts, shall hold their offices during good behaviour, and shall, at stated times, receive for their services, a compensation, which shall not be diminished during their continuance in office.

Section 2. The judicial power shall extend to all cases, in law and equity, arising under this Constitution, the laws of the United States, and treaties made, or which shall be made, under their authority;—to all cases affecting ambassadors, other public ministers and consuls;—to all cases of admiralty and maritime jurisdiction, [—to controversies to which the United States shall be a party;— to controversies between two or more states, [between a state and citizens of another state;], between citizens of different states;—between citizens of the same state, claiming lands under grants of different states, and between a state, or the citizens thereof, and foreign states, [citizens or subjects].

In all cases affecting ambassadors, other public ministers and consuls, and those in which a state shall be party, the Supreme Court shall have original jurisdiction. In all the other cases before mentioned, the Supreme Court shall have appellate jurisdiction, both as to law and fact, with such exceptions, and under such regulations as the Congress shall make.

The trial of all crimes, except in cases of impeachment, shall be by jury; and such trial shall be held in the state where the said crimes shall have been committed; but when not committed within any state, the trial shall be at such place or places as the Congress may by law have directed.

Section 3. Treason against the United States, shall consist only in levying war against them, or in adhering to their enemies, giving them aid and comfort. No person shall be convicted of treason unless on the testimony of two witnesses to the same overt act, or on confession in open court.

The Congress shall have power to declare the punishment of treason, but no attainder of treason shall work corruption of blood, or forfeiture except during the life of the person attainted.

Article IV
Relation of the States to Each Other

Section 1. Full faith and credit shall be given in each state to the public acts, records, and judicial proceedings of every other state. And the Congress may by general laws prescribe the manner in which such acts, records, and proceedings shall be proved, and the effect thereof.

Section 2. The citizens of each state shall be entitled to all privileges and immunities of citizens in the several states.

A person charged in any state with treason, felony, or other crime, who shall flee from justice, and be found in another state, shall on demand of the executive authority of the state from which he fled, be delivered up, to be removed to the state having jurisdiction of the crime.

[No person held to service or labor in one state, under the laws thereof, escaping into another, shall, in consequence of any law or regulation therein, be discharged from such service or labor, but shall be delivered up on claim of the party to whom such service or labor may be due.]

Federal-State Relations

Section 3. New states may be admitted by the Congress into this Union; but no new states shall be formed or erected within the jurisdiction of any other state, nor any state be formed by the junction of two or more states, without the consent of the legislatures of the states concerned, as well as of the Congress.

The Congress shall have power to dispose of and make all needful rules and regulations respecting the territory or other property belonging to the United States; and nothing in this Constitution shall be so construed as to prejudice any claims of the United States, or of any particular state.

Section 4. The United States shall guarantee to every state in this union a republican form of government, and shall protect each of them against invasion; and on application of the legislature, or of the executive (when the legislature cannot be convened) against domestic violence.

Article V
Amending the Constitution

The Congress, whenever two thirds of both houses shall deem it necessary, shall propose amendments to this Constitution, or, on the application of the legislatures of two thirds of the several states, shall call a convention for proposing amendments, which, in either case, shall be valid to all intents and purposes, as part of this Constitution, when ratified by the legislatures of three fourths of the several states, or by conventions in three fourths thereof, as the one or the other mode of ratification may be proposed by the Congress; provided [that no amendment which may be made prior to the year one thousand eight hundred and eight shall in any manner affect the first and fourth clauses in the ninth section of the first article; and] that no state, without its consent, shall be deprived of its equal suffrage in the Senate.

Article VI
National Debts

All debts contracted and engagements entered into, before the adoption of this Constitution, shall be as valid against the United States under this Constitution, as under the Confederation.

Supremacy of the National Government

This Constitution, and the laws of the United States which shall be made in pursuance thereof; and all treaties made, or which shall be made, under the authority of the United States, shall be the supreme law of the land; and the judges in every state shall be bound thereby, anything in the constitution or laws of any State to the contrary notwithstanding.

The senators and representatives before mentioned, and the members of the several state legislatures, and all executive and judicial officers, both of the United States and of the several states, shall be bound by oath or affirmation, to support this Constitution; but no religious test shall ever be required as a qualification to any office or public trust under the United States.

Article VII
Ratifying the Constitution

The ratification of the conventions of nine states, shall be sufficient for the establishment of this Constitution between the states so ratifying the same.

Done in convention by the unanimous consent of the states present the seventeenth day of September in the year of our Lord one thousand seven hundred and eighty seven and of the independence of the United States of America the twelfth. In witness whereof we have hereunto subscribed our Names.

Amendment I

Congress shall make no law respecting an establishment of religion, or prohibiting the free exercise thereof; or abridging the freedom of speech, or of the press; or the right of the people peaceably to assemble, and to petition the Government for a redress of grievances.

Report Links

The Internet sites described below can be accessed at
http://www.myreportlinks.com

▶ **The Charters of Freedom: Bill of Rights**
Editor's Choice See a copy of the first ten amendments to the Constitution, known as the Bill of Rights.

▶ **U.S. Constitution: First Amendment**
Editor's Choice Gain an appreciation for First Amendment freedoms at this site.

▶ **Ben's Guide to U.S. Government for Kids**
Editor's Choice Learn how the three branches of the federal government work together.

▶ **American Library Association**
Editor's Choice Find out what libraries do to fight censorship and promote free speech.

▶ **First Amendment Center**
Editor's Choice Read about First Amendment freedoms.

▶ **The Supreme Court of the United States**
Editor's Choice Learn about the history and inner-workings of the highest court in the land.

▶ **Alien and Sedition Acts**
Explore an important if short-lived effort to restrict a type of speech.

▶ **Alliance Defense Fund**
Discover the efforts of a leading advocacy group that fights for freedom of religious expression.

▶ **American Civil Liberties Union**
Learn about this group's efforts to protect Americans' First Amendment rights.

▶ **Americans United for Separation of Church and State**
Read the views of a group that seeks to foster a strong separation of church and state.

▶ **Anti-Defamation League**
Explore the role of religion in public schools with experts from the Anti-Defamation League.

▶ **The Anti-Federalist Papers**
Read the concerns of early Americans who feared that a new federal union would erode their freedoms.

▶ **The Center for Education Reform**
Learn the perspective of a group that supports charter schools and school vouchers.

▶ **English Bill of Rights**
Read a seventeenth-century document that influenced the development of the U.S Constitution.

▶ **Exploring Constitutional Conflicts**
Learn both sides of the controversy over flag burning.

Report Links

The Internet sites described below can be accessed at http://www.myreportlinks.com

▶**Faith-Based and Community Initiatives**
Examine President George W. Bush's efforts to promote faith-based and community initiatives.

▶*The Federalist:* **A Collection of Essays**
Read *The Federalist Papers,* important documents in the development of the U.S. Constitution.

▶**Frequently Asked Questions about Defamation**
Learn about libel and defamation and how they relate to freedom of speech.

▶**National Education Association: Vouchers**
Read the views of the nation's largest teachers' union, which opposes public support of private education.

▶**The National Security Archive: The Pentagon Papers**
Browse documents from a case that greatly impacted freedom of the press.

▶**Obscenity, Indecency and Profanity**
Take a look at the federal government's oversight of speech in broadcast media.

▶**Privacy.Org**
Learn about issues of privacy and freedom of assembly in the digital age.

▶**Religion and the Founding of the American Republic**
Learn how religion factored into the founding of the United States.

▶**The Rutherford Institute: Free Speech**
Find out what the Rutherford Group is doing to promote free speech and religious liberties.

▶*Schenck* v. *United States*
Read *Schenck* v. *U.S.* to learn why falsely shouting "fire" in a theater isn't protected speech.

▶**The U.S. Constitution with Explanatory Notes**
Learn about the history and provisions of the Constitution of the United States.

▶**U.S. Supreme Court Obscenity Decisions**
Review more than a century's worth records to learn how the courts have addressed obscenity.

▶**The Virginia Declaration of Rights**
Learn how the Virginia Declaration of Rights impacted the Declaration of Independence.

▶**The White House: James Madison**
Read a biography of an early president and framer of the Constitution of the United States.

▶**The Zenger Trial: An Account**
Read about an important early court case dealing with freedom of speech.

censorship—The removal of information from the public, or the prevention of circulation of information.

compel—To cause to do or occur by overwhelming pressure.

defamation—Making a false claim that may harm the reputation of an individual, business, group, product, or government.

desecrate—To treat disrespectfully or outrageously.

directed verdict—A jury verdict ordered by a judge because one side in a court case did not prove his or her case as matter of law.

free association—A legal concept based on the idea that adults are allowed to associate with any other adult they choose.

liable—A person or entity that is responsible, as in, to pay a debt.

libel—To publish, write, or broadcast an untrue statement intended to harm the reputation of a person.

misdemeanor—A crime less serious than a felony; misdemeanors generally have smaller fines or jail time of less than a year.

obscenity—Typically defined as indecency, lewdness, or offensiveness in behavior, expression, or appearance. Obscenity is difficult to assess from a legal perspective: What is offensive to one person may not be offensive to another.

per curiam—A decision issued from the Supreme Court as a whole rather than one written and signed by an individual justice.

pornography—Material like books and photographs that shows behavior that is intended to cause sexual excitement.

prior restraint—A court order banning the publication and dissemination of previously unpublished material.

principle—A comprehensive and fundamental law; a rule or code of conduct.

privilege—A special benefit or immunity from penalty given to a particular person or group.

restraining order—A temporary court order to keep conditions as they are until a court hearing can be held.

sedition—Inciting contempt or rebellion against a government.

slander—An untrue, spoken statement intended to harm a person's reputation.

subpoena—A court order requiring a person to appear before the court at a particular time.

uphold—To maintain or defend something, especially laws or principles.

Chapter 1. The First Amendment in Action

1. Tiffany Hsu, "Balco reporters to discuss brush with First Amendment," *ASNE Reporter 2007,* March 26, 2007, <http://www.asne.org/print.cfm?printer _page=%2Findex.cfm%3FID%3D6494> (June 20, 2008).

2. Paul Starr, *The Creation of the Media, Political Origins of Modern Communications* (New York: Basic Books 2004), pp. 58–59.

3. Ibid, p. 59.

4. *The Crown* v. *John Peter Zenger,* trial transcript, pp. 71–72.

Chapter 2. The Origins of the Amendment

1. Akhil Reed Amar, *The Bill of Rights* (New Haven, Conn.: Yale University Press, 1998), pp. 24–25.

2. Alexander Hamilton, James Madison, and John Jay, *The Federalist Papers* (New York: Bantam Classics, 2003), pp. ix–xiii.

3. Ibid, p. 524.

4. Ralph Ketcham, *The Anti-Federalist Papers* (New York: Signet Classic, 2003), pp. 195–196.

5. Edmund S. Morgan, *The Birth of the Republic* (Chicago: The University of Chicago Press, 1992), pp. 152–153.

6. Jack N. Rakove, *Founding America, Documents from the Revolution to the Bill of Rights* (New York: Barnes & Noble Classics, 2006), pp. 302–303.

Chapter 3. The Amendment Up Close

1. *Barron* v. *Baltimore,* 32 U.S. 243 (1833).

2. *Gitlow* v. *New York,* 268 U.S. 652 (1925).

Chapter 4. Separation of Church and State

1. *Bradfield* v. *Roberts,* 175 U.S. 291 (1899).

2. *Everson* v. *Board of Education,* 330 U.S. 1 (1947).

3. *Illinois ex rel McCollum* v. *Board of Education,* 333 U.S. 203 (1948).

4. Ibid.

5. *Zorach* v. *Clauson,* 343 U.S. 306 (1952).

6. *Walz* v. *Tax Commission,* 397 U.S. 664 (1970).

7. *Lemon* v. *Kurtzman,* 403 U.S. 602 (1971).

8. Ibid.

9. *Engal* v. *Vitale,* 370 U.S. 421 (1962).

10. *Abington Township School District* v. *Schempp,* 374 U.S. 203 (1963).

11. *Wallace* v. *Jaffree,* 472 U.S. 38 (1985).

12. *County of Allegheny* v. *ACLU,* 492 U.S. 573 (1989).

13. *Reynolds* v. *United States,* 98 U.S. 145 (1878).

14. *Cantwell* v. *Connecticut,* 310 U.S. 296 (1940).

Chapter 5. Freedom of Speech

1. Akhil Reed Amar, *The Bill of Rights* (New Haven, Conn.: Yale University Press, 1998), p. 23.

2. *Schenck* v. *United States,* 249 U.S. 47 (1919).

3. Ibid.

4. *Gitlow* v. *New York,* 268 U.S. 652 (1925).

5. 18 U.S.C. sec. 2385 (2000).

6. *Dennis* v. *United States,* 341 U.S. 494 (1951).

7. Ibid.

8. *Yates* v. *United States,* 354 U.S. 298 (1957).

9. *Brandenburg* v. *Ohio,* 395 U.S. 444 (1969).

10. *Texas* v. *Johnson,* 491 U.S. 397 (1989).

11. *United States* v. *Eichman,* 496 U.S. 310 (1990).

12. *Roth* v. *United States,* 354 U.S. 496 (1957).

13. *Miller* v. *California,* 413 U.S. 15 (1973).

14. *New York* v. *Ferber,* 458 U.S. 747 (1982).

15. *Stanley* v. *Georgia,* 394 U.S. 557 (1969).

16. *New York Times Co.* v. *Sullivan,* 376 U.S. 254 (1964).

17. *Milkovich* v. *Lorain Journal Co.,* 497 U.S. 1 (1990).

18. *Branzburg* v. *Hayes,* 408 U.S. 665 (1972).

19. *Miami Herald Publishing Co.* v. *Tornillo,* 418 U.S. 241 (1974).

Chapter 6. The Constitution Evolves

1. *Zelman* v. *Simmons-Harris,* 536 U.S. 639 (2002).

2. *Lee* v. *Weisman,* 505 U.S. 577 (1992).

3. *Santa Fe Independent School District* v. *Doe,* 530 U.S. 290 (2000).

4. *Van Orden* v. *Perry,* 545 U.S. 647 (2005).

5. *McCreary County* v. *ACLU of Kentucky,* 545 U.S. 844 (2005).

6. *Ashcroft* v. *Free Speech Coalition,* 535 U.S. 224 (2002).

7. Linda Greenhouse, "Supreme Court Upholds Child Pornography Law," *The New York Times,* May 20, 2008, <http://www.nytimes.com/2008/05/20/washington/20scotus.html?pagewanted=print> (June 20, 2008).

8. *Bartnicki* v. *Vopper,* 532 U.S. 514 (2001).

9. *Boy Scouts of America* v. *Dale,* 530 U.S. 640 (2000).

Allport, Alan. *Freedom of Speech*. Philadelphia: Chelsea House Publishers, 2003.

Friedman, Ian C. *Freedom of Speech and the Press*. New York: Facts On File, 2005.

Gottfried, Todd. *Homeland Security vs. Constitutional Rights*. Brookfield, Conn.: 21st Century Books, 2003.

Head, Tom. *Freedom of Religion*. New York: Facts on File, 2005.

Herumin, Wendy. *Censorship on the Internet: From Filters to Freedom of Speech*. Berkeley Heights, N.J.: Enslow Publishers, 2004.

Hudson, David L. *The Bill of Rights: The First Ten Amendments of the Constitution*. Berkeley Heights, N.J.: Enslow Publishers, 2002.

Isler, Claudia. *The Right to Free Speech*. New York: Rosen Pub. Group, 2001.

Pendergast, Sara, Tom Pendergast, and John Sousanis. *Constitutional Amendments: From Freedom of Speech to Flag Burning*. Detroit: UXL, 2001.

Weidner, Daniel. *The Constitution: The Preamble and the Articles*. Berkeley Heights, N.J.: Enslow Publishers, 2002.